DIVE ENGLAND'S GREATEST WRECKS

Also by Rod Macdonald

Dive Scapa Flow, first published 1990. Third edition 1998.
Dive Scotland's Greatest Wrecks, first published 1993, second edition 2000.

DIVE England's Greatest Wrecks

Rod Macdonald

MAINSTREAM
PUBLISHING
EDINBURGH AND LONDON

First published in Great Britain in 2003 by
MAINSTREAM PUBLISHING (EDINBURGH) LTD
7 Albany Street
Edinburgh EH1 3UG

ISBN 1 84018 570 8

A catalogue record for this book is available from the British Library

Typeset in Baskerville MT and Stone Print

Printed in Great Britain by
Antony Rowe Ltd, Chippenham, Wiltshire

TO MY MOTHER AND FATHER

Contents

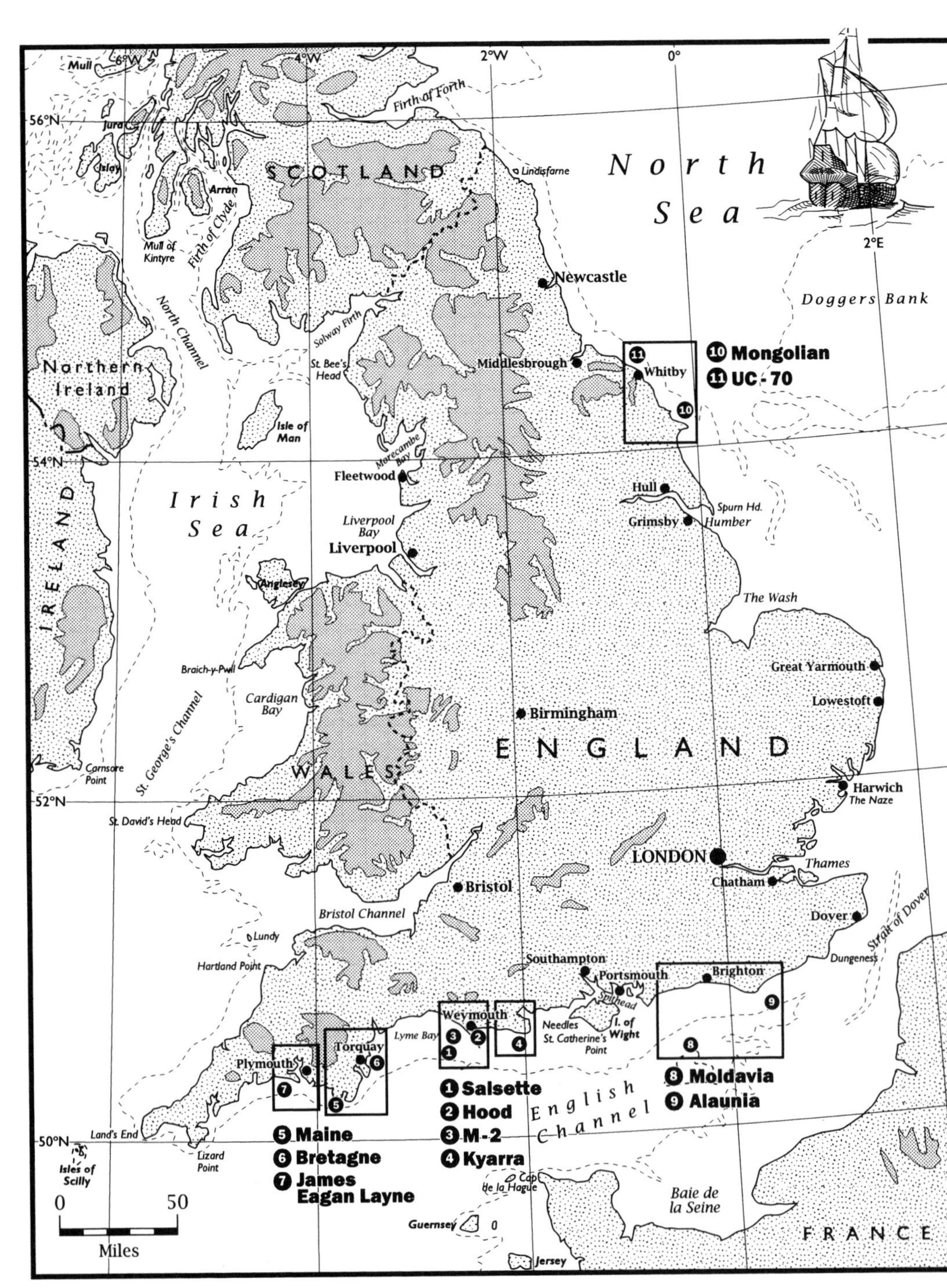

Mull
6°W
4°W
2°W
0°
56°N
Jura
Islay
Arran
Mull of Kintyre
Firth of Clyde
Firth of Forth
SCOTLAND
Lindisfarne
North Sea
2°E
Newcastle
Doggers Bank
North Channel
Solway Firth
Northern Ireland
St Bee's Head
Middlesbrough
Whitby
⑩ Mongolian
⑪ UC-70
Isle of Man
Morecambe Bay
54°N
Fleetwood
Irish Sea
Hull
Spurn Hd.
Grimsby
Humber
Liverpool Bay
Liverpool
IRELAND
Anglesey
The Wash
Braich-y-Pwll
Great Yarmouth
Cardigan Bay
Birmingham
Lowestoft
St. George's Channel
ENGLAND
Carnsore Point
WALES
Harwich
The Naze
52°N
St David's Head
LONDON
Thames
Bristol
Chatham
Bristol Channel
Dover
Strait of Dover
Lundy
Hartland Point
Southampton
Portsmouth
Brighton
Dungeness
Spithead
Weymouth
Lyme Bay
Needles
St. Catherine's Point
I. of Wight
Torquay
Plymouth
English Channel
① Salsette
② Hood
③ M-2
④ Kyarra
⑤ Maine
⑥ Bretagne
⑦ James Eagan Layne
⑧ Moldavia
⑨ Alaunia
Land's End
50°N
Isles of Scilly
Lizard Point
0
50
Miles
Cap de la Hague
Baie de la Seine
Guernsey
Jersey
FRANCE

ACKNOWLEDGEMENTS

It had been almost eight years since the publication of my second book, *Dive Scotland's Greatest Wrecks*. I had been involved in other projects, such as expanding that book for the 2000 second edition and expanding my first book, *Dive Scapa Flow*, for its 1998 third edition, but I longed for the challenge of writing a complete new book on shipwrecks. When I thought of the idea of a complementary book about great English shipwrecks I should have been more aware of the enormity of the project I was taking on.

Rashly I gave myself only one year to research and dive ten of the greatest shipwrecks in English waters and to complete the manuscript and hand it in to my understanding publishers, Mainstream Publishing of Edinburgh. However, for someone living in the north of Scotland, the difficult logistics of the project soon became apparent. These wrecks were far away from me and spread out along the English Channel and up to Yorkshire. At least when I wrote *Dive Scapa Flow* all the wrecks were bunched together in an area 15 miles across. To survey all these wrecks in English waters was going to take a number of time-consuming, arduous and expensive trips down to England.

I arranged the first of these trips to the English Channel for the beginning of May 2002. As history now bears witness, Britain had a terrible start to the year with stormy sea conditions right up to the end of May. My helpful spies in the English Channel, such as Doc David Adey, fed me regular visibility reports. In the days leading up to this first

OPPOSITE: ENGLAND'S GREATEST SHIPWRECKS

trip I was being told, 'The weather is foul – and the underwater visibility is 1 metre. Don't come.'

It was impossible to contemplate surveying P&O liners, in excess of 500 feet in length, in any detail when I would be floundering about in 1-metre pitch-black visibility. Bravely, or foolishly, I resolved to tough it out and go. The latest weather reports were so bad on the morning of my planned departure, however, that I had to give in to the inevitable and cancel the trip only 30 minutes before I was due to depart. Hastily I rearranged the first trip for later in May, but the bad weather continued and the visibility, now affected by the plankton bloom, the 'May Waters', didn't get any better. Like the first scheduled trip, this one also had to be cancelled at the last moment. Although I had spent the winter researching and writing the histories of the wrecks, I only had four months to go until the manuscript was due in to my publishers and I still had not seen or touched any of the wrecks.

Then my luck changed. I had rearranged the trip yet again, this time for June; the weather improved and the trip was on. I drove down from Stonehaven, near Aberdeen, with my car packed full of dive kit, tanks, video cameras and an underwater scooter and arrived full of anticipation at Budgie's Aqua Hotel in Portland, where I would be based. An old dive mate of mine from the Aberdeen area, Steve Collard, now lived and worked in London and was coming down to join me for the week the next day. Budgie runs a good, well-organised dive operation from Portland and couldn't have been more helpful. I was able, within hours of arriving, to get a dive in on HMS *Hood*, a pre-dreadnought battleship sunk across the entrance to Portland harbour as a blockship during the First World War. With my underwater video camera mounted on my Aquazepp underwater scooter I was able to cover this wreck in detail and get a good feel for her. Things were looking up.

Steve arrived that night. The following day we were off early to dive the British submarine *M2*. Later that day we got a second dive on HMS *Hood*, which helped with my understanding of her layout. The next day we were out diving the beautiful wreck of the *Salsette*. With a bottom time of almost half an hour on her at 45 metres, we were able to get round the whole wreck easily on our scooters.

That week we were able to dive and survey one glorious wreck after another. In the evening of the *Salsette* dive we drove to Swanage and got out to dive the *Kyarra*. The next day saw us driving to Babbacombe, where we got out with the very helpful Divers Down of Torquay to survey the haunting remains of SS *Bretagne*.

Towards the end of the week, the fine weather started to break but we headed down to Plymouth and were able to charter a boat from our friends at Deep

Blue and get out to dive and survey the SS *Maine*, perhaps my favourite of all the English wrecks. Then, just as the weather broke, we surveyed the hugely popular Second World War Liberty ship, *James Eagan Layne*, in atrocious weather conditions. Had we committed to either the week before or the week after this fine weather window, we would have been blown out. We had been lucky.

I hugely enjoyed my time diving these fantastic wrecks out of Portland and Plymouth. I liked the whole dive-orientated atmosphere down there – it is a diver's world and we met many interesting characters. Part of the pleasure of these trips *is* the people that you meet. You soon realise what a small world the diving one is. Nearly everyone you talk to knows someone you have dived with. The diving community is a global village.

Once back in Scotland I could get down to writing the diving sections on the wrecks I had now surveyed and start planning my next trip down south. September came and it was time to head up towards Eastbourne at the Eastern end of the English Channel where, once again accompanied by Steve Collard, we were able to get out and survey the wrecks of the *Moldavia* and *Alaunia*. It was a week of much driving, good diving and little sleep. Finally, in October, I was able to get down to Filey Bay in Yorkshire and research the First World War wrecks of the *Mongolian* and the German submarine *UC-70* which sunk her – and coincidentally ended up being sunk herself a few months later, not far away.

My heartfelt thanks must therefore go out to Steve Collard who bravely put up with my dragging him to far-flung parts of the English Channel. Steve had recently purchased an Aquazepp underwater scooter like mine, so the two of us were able to move quickly over the wrecks frantically trying to take in what we were seeing. If the visibility was good I mounted my video camera on my Zepp and filmed as we scootered over the wreck. If it was poor the video was no use and I manually sketched as we went along.

Steve is an immensely capable technical diver and that ability, allied with his technical knowledge of ships and engineering, was a huge help in understanding the layout of these wrecks. It is fair to say that we did not have a single mishap in all these dives other than a single simple reel jam. In sometimes very poor visibility we only managed to get separated on one occasion – but very quickly we were able to follow the sound of our scooters and home in on each other.

In Portland, Budgie was very helpful, both for his knowledge of the wrecks and sea conditions, and for squeezing his scheduled dives to accommodate us. It was much appreciated. In Plymouth it was Phil Hodson of Deep Blue, whom I knew from his days at Aberdeen Watersports, my local dive shop, who set things up for us and helped when he could.

My thanks must also go to David Hunter and the fellow members of the Filey Bay BSAC. David went to a lot of time and trouble for me when I was researching the wrecks of the *Mongolian* and *UC-70* down in Filey along with my fellow Scottish divers Richard Colliar and Martin Sinclair. Again, it was much appreciated. Only Filey Bay BSAC know the true story behind the chapter on the *Mongolian* – and I am relying on them to keep it to themselves!

It is a testament to the former strength of Glasgow and the Clyde as a world centre for shipbuilding that many of these wrecks, although lying in English waters, were actually built on the Clyde. My old dive mate Peter Moir is the co-author of two essential books on Scottish shipwrecks, *Clyde Shipwrecks* and *Argyll Shipwrecks*. He is the fount of all knowledge when it comes to Clyde-built ships and helpfully he was able to provide me instantly with details on many of the shipbuilders.

David Jarvie is a Royal Navy submariner who coincidentally lives in the same town as myself, Stonehaven. He took an immediate interest in the *M2* and was able to point me in the right direction during my research on that tragic vessel. Again my thanks go out to him.

As with my two previous books, *Dive Scapa Flow* and *Dive Scotland's Greatest Wrecks*, my regular dive buddy and soulmate Ewan Rowell provided the stunning underwater shot that ended up on the cover of this book.

Our attempts to dive the massive Sussex wreck *Alaunia* seemed at first also to have been blown out by the weather. We turned up at Newhaven Marina for a 7 a.m. departure only to find out that the weather was too bad and the skipper of the chartered dive boat wouldn't go to sea. There was a very dejected party of divers, some of whom had driven down from London that morning for the dive, left standing on the pier as the skipper disappeared over the horizon. The weather was due to settle later in the day and by luck we managed to get hold of the well-run, Eastbourne-based *Taurus* boat charter. They agreed to take us out at 4 p.m. that day. The conditions settled and we had 45 glorious minutes down on the wreck of the *Alaunia* before a long decompression hang on our delayed deco buoys. By the time we got back near shore, darkness had fallen and the navigation beacons winked as they guided us back to the safety of the Marina.

Mark Dyer has just set up Planet Dive at Eastbourne Marina, a first-class Technical Diving Inc. (TDI) technical facility. We had talked to Mark earlier in the day to let him know we'd be back ashore late. Mark was fantastically helpful and arranged to come back to his shop that night as we appeared wet and bedraggled out of the darkness, twin sets slung over our backs. He opened up his shop and sorted out Trimix fills for us for the next day's dive on the *Moldavia* – and also gave us very welcome use of his shower unit whilst the fills were being made. We reciprocated by taking him out for a very pleasant pizza and beers in the Marina. I wish him every success with his dive centre.

After pizza, it was time for a late dash to Littlehampton where we unfortunately woke up the landlady of the B&B we were staying at. She had been warned that we were going to be late but must have given up on us. It felt like our heads had barely hit the pillow before our alarms were going off and it was time to get up and breakfast in time to get down to the Marina for a 7 a.m. departure on Paul and Kelly Child's very slick *Voyager* dive operation. *Voyager* and its new companion vessel, *Defiant*, are well-equipped, spacious and fast dive boats. Ours, *Defiant*, made the 26-mile trip out to the wreck of the *Moldavia* very comfortable.

Tim Clouter and Stewart Butterfield were able to help me with the wreck of the *Bretagne*, which has been close to their hearts for a long time. Their information and assistance were most appreciated.

After Filey Bay, it was simply a case of getting down to the grind of finishing off the book. We had ridden our luck and got the breaks as we pitched up in a rush at one dive location after another, just as the skies cleared and the seas settled.

As I write about my experiences, the overwhelming impression I am left with of my time down in England is of the kindness and helpfulness so freely shown to me by everyone I turned to for assistance. I look forward to returning to spend some more time exploring these amazing wrecks again. As with my two previous books, once I had dived the wrecks and assimilated all the information I was able to brief my artist, Rob Ward of Illusion Illustration Ltd, Bridge of Muchalls, Kincardineshire. Rob, a non-diver, has once again been fantastic in helping me piece together the stunning impressions of what the complete wreck looks like on the seabed. Non-divers should be aware however that the wreck impressions are not what a diver sees – at best a diver will see from 5–50 feet of the wreck at any one time, depending on underwater visibility. The paintings are intended to provide on paper an impression of what the wrecks are like, which will help visiting divers plan their dives and allow non-divers a glimpse of what the wreck, hidden to them by the sea, actually looks like.

Ian Williamson once again was able to listen to my layman's ideas for charts and cutaway drawings and with his skill and ability tell me what would work and what wouldn't. He was able to crystallise my ideas, and the finished work he has produced is exceptional and of the highest quality. It is only by talking to Ian in depth that I have gained an understanding of how much work goes into just one of these charts. Thank you again, Ian.

No set of acknowledgements would be complete without a thank you to my wife Claire and my two daughters, Nicola and Catriona. Claire was helpful and encouraging and lifted my spirits when the going got tough. She came up with a lot of good ideas that I was able to use. Nicola and Catriona refrained from jumping all over me for rough and tumble long enough at times to let me do some typing.

So many other people have contributed in other essential ways. Gerry Hassell, the MD of GH Engineering and Diving Services, North Feltham, London, is Chairman of the Kingston and Elmbridge branch of the BSAC. He helped me with hire kit and at the drop of a hat was very easily able to drill my stainless steel backplate for my scooter harness to accommodate differing tanks. The staff at Stonehaven Public Library fielded my requests for obscure and long out-of-print reference books; they were very helpful, as were the Imperial War Museum, the National Maritime Museum and Aberdeen Maritime Museum.

I am relieved that this book has finally hit the bookshelves. It has been touch and go all the way and has involved a lot of hard work and time. This will probably be the last pure wreck-diving book of this ilk that I will write. My thoughts are already turning to my next book, a non-fiction collection of diving stories, *Into the Abyss*, which is scheduled for publication later this year.

I hope that you enjoy reading this book and, that if you are to dive any of these wrecks, you enjoy them as much as I did.

Good diving!

Rod Macdonald, 2003

Author's Technical Note

Ship's capacities for cargo-carrying were calculated in tonnage, of which several variations existed although a general calculation was that the ton-register was 100 cubic feet. The various tonnages that are used throughout this book are as follows:

GROSS TONNAGE: This was all of a vessel's enclosed space (i.e. including crew's quarters, engine-room etc.) divided by 100.

NET TONNAGE: This was the gross tonnage, as above, less spaces not used for cargo or passengers.

DEAD-WEIGHT TONNAGE: The number of tons (of 2,240lb) of cargo and fuel coal that a ship could carry when loaded to the waterline; calculated by multiplying gross tonnage by 1.6.

DISPLACEMENT TONNAGE: The number of tons of sea water displaced by the ship when it was loaded to the load waterline.

All depths and modern diving-related measurements are given in metres of sea water (msw). However, all references to ship's dimensions etc. are given in the Imperial measurements, feet and inches, of the time of their construction.

INTRODUCTION

The English Channel, the narrow stretch of water that divides Britain from mainland Europe, has for centuries been a natural barrier which helped protect our island nation from enemies that might seek to conquer it.

From the earliest times, the Channel, just 21 miles wide at its narrowest point, has seen countless and immensely varied types of shipping passing up and down. It is now, by virtue of the volume of sea traffic using it, justly recognised as the busiest sea channel in the world. So busy is it, that strict lanes north and south have been created to try and separate north- and south-bound shipping – much like a motorway.

With such a volume of shipping it is not surprising that the Channel teems with relics of shipping disasters, legacies of unfortunate accidents. Countless vessels have been sent to lie at the bottom of the Channel, victims of collision, human error or simple bad luck. But it is the spectre of war that has ironically given the Channel its greatest underwater legacy. During the two great World Wars of the twentieth century the English Channel again assumed its role as a natural barrier, but one not so insurmountable as in the past when the Spanish or Napoleon had eyed our land keenly. Britain fortified the Channel in both wars with as many sea defences as possible in an effort to give some measure of protection to the vulnerable merchant or civilian vessels that were a vital part of the war effort.

In the First World War great barriers of steel nets were stretched across militarily critical areas – anti-submarine nets to prevent the new and much-feared U-boat menace from operating and targeting Allied shipping. The Belgian coastal barrage ran from Dunkirk north to the Scheldt, a distance of some 35 miles. The Dover nets ran from the Goodwins to the Snou Bank. A further set of nets blocked the short bottleneck stretch from Folkestone to Cap Gris Nez, on the northern French coast.

From these great steel net walls, mines were hung at differing depths to try and snare the unwary U-boat. Mines could be set off by simple contact. Other systems employed acoustic detector loops that fed information back to distant operators who could detonate mines remotely if a foe was thought to be close. Giant shore-based searchlights could reach out to mid-Channel, lighting up the darkness of night as though it were day should a raider be detected. Sleek, fast patrol boats, ever watchful for the sight of a U-boat on the surface trying to slip over the nets, were ready to pounce and attack or depth charge.

Despite the massive scale of these defences, U-boats frequently managed to run the net and mine barrages, finding the freedom to operate in the more open waters of the southern section of the Channel. The sea war was indeed cruel. U-boats sent many Allied vessels in both wars to the bottom, and the U-boats themselves were very susceptible to detection and attack. The average life expectancy of a U-boat submariner in the First World War was just six trips. Often the hunter U-boat found itself detected and in turn became the prey, hunted to a terrifying finale in the dark depths of the Channel's cold waters.

It is the legacy of those cruel wars that now lies in the depths of the English Channel. A glance at the Admiralty Charts reveals a legion of wrecks wherever you look. It is too easy to forget that each simple wreck symbol on a chart represents a traumatic and terrifying event that often took young lives, left others permanently disabled, created countless widows, and left children who would never enjoy a father's love.

Each wreck symbol represents the shock of a catastrophic torpedo or mine explosion. It symbolises a gripping, paralysing fear – the sudden realisation that a seemingly unsinkable ship, a familiar home often for a very long time, was now shortly to slip beneath the waves. It recalls the dread fear of the survivors as their ship plunged them into icy seas, at the mercy of nature. Survivors needed to be plucked from the water quickly were they not to succumb to hypothermia and the strong Channel currents. The scars of these sinkings would last a lifetime – a love lost and never replaced, a sad mother, sitting alone, longingly reading her lost son's letters, years after the war had ended. Sometimes the loss of a loved one was never accepted. Sad tales abound, like that of a mother leaving the door of the family home open for years after a sinking in the belief that her son was not dead, that one day he would walk in through that door. Forget not what each wreck symbol means.

The number of wreck symbols in the English Channel is quite startling and it is hard to appreciate the scale of the shipping losses that have occurred here. West Bay, where the unique submarine *M2* was lost off Portland in 1932, was long ago known as The Bay of a Thousand Wrecks – and that was before the onset of the Second World War, with the carnage that brought and the legacy of wrecks it left.

In wartime, shipping coming across the Atlantic or up from Africa or the Empire was at its most vulnerable when it entered the English Channel at journey's end, heading for the Channel ports. Equally when Allied shipping left the protection of the home ports, perhaps departing with troops or supplies for the European battlefields, it became a target for the U-boats or air attack. It is therefore not surprising that the vast majority of the wrecks in this book are to be found spread out along the length of the Channel – relics of those hostilities.

During both World Wars, Scapa Flow, in the Orkney Islands of northern Scotland, was a heavily guarded anchorage for Royal Navy vessels, and by necessity there was much shipping movement between the Flow and the Channel. In addition, convoys and freighters often had to pass up and down the east coast of Britain, whether arriving from America and Canada with war supplies or inbound from Africa or other parts of the world with supplies, armaments, foodstuffs or raw materials. Vessels from Africa and the like, destined for London and the east coast ports of England, often would not risk the dangers associated with passing through the Channel from the south but would make the laborious journey up the west coast of Britain, before heeling to the east, past Orkney, and then passing down the east coast. As a result, on the passage down the east coast ships were vulnerable to attack by German U-boats and additionally, in the Second World War, by German aircraft.

By way of example of that, for Chapter Ten I have chosen the First World War wreck of the SS *Mongolian*. This 4,838-ton single-screw steamer, on a voyage from Middlesbrough down the east coast to London, found herself attacked by *UC-70*, a small U-boat designed to operate in shallow coastal areas, where her main role was as a mine-layer. A torpedo from *UC-70* struck the *Mongolian* and sent her to the bottom of Filey Bay, Yorkshire. Ironically, *UC-70* herself, although she escaped unscathed from that fatal attack, returned some months later to the same killing ground. This time the fates were against her. She was detected and sunk off Whitby, not far away from the *Mongolian*'s resting place in Filey Bay. There is something tragic and futile in both the hunted and the hunter ending their days in the uncaring grip of the same cruel stretch of sea.

In the Second World War, to try and give coastal shipping passing up and down the east coast between London and Scapa Flow a degree of protection from enemy operations such as those that had sent the *Mongolian* to the bottom 20 years earlier, a channel running the full length of the eastern coastline of Britain was marked out some eight miles offshore. This channel, which was regularly swept for enemy mines laid by U-boats or surface vessels, began at Duncansby Head, the very north-east tip of Scotland, and ran down to the Thames Estuary. It was approximately half- to one-mile wide and was marked with buoys every ten miles.

The Northern Mine Barrage was laid in a line from the Thames Estuary northwards, initially up to Fraserburgh in north-east Scotland, latterly being extended to run up to Orkney. This defensive Mine Barrage was deployed further out in the North Sea than the swept channel and was designed to protect coastal shipping against enemy surface vessels and submarines. Notwithstanding the huge effort in setting up this undertaking, Allied shipping suffered heavily at the hands of German U-boats and aircraft. The North Sea is littered with the wrecks of those vessels.

The 5,842-ton P&O express mail liner *Salsette* is a wreck that many divers regard as the greatest wreck in English waters. Lying in 44msw and largely intact, she rests on her port side a few miles out of Portland harbour. She is a fascinating glimpse back to the era of straight-stem steamers and with frequent good underwater visibility of 10–20 metres, justly opens the book in Chapter One.

As a complete contrast to the *Salsette*, for Chapter Two I have chosen the wreck of the colossal 1891 pre-dreadnought battleship HMS *Hood* which was scuttled across the entrance to Portland harbour in 1914 as a blockship. The construction and deployment of HMS *Dreadnought* in 1906 had overnight rendered the pre-dreadnought battleships obsolete. Her time past, HMS *Hood* was one of the first pre-dreadnoughts to go onto reserve duties in 1905. She is however a tantalising glimpse of a monstrous leviathan from pre-dreadnought days – a time capsule forever destined to guard the approaches to Portland harbour.

For Chapter Three, I have chosen another very special wreck in the Portland area, the British submarine *M2*. She was a unique and experimental submarine built at the close of the First World War. Initially she was fitted out with a single 12-inch battleship gun in a turret forward of the conning tower. In the post-war years, however, this was removed and in its place, in a formidable piece of innovative thinking, a watertight aeroplane hangar was fitted, large enough to house the smallest seaplane in the world. This innovation gave a far-ranging capability to the submarine, but sadly would also lead to its tragic loss with all hands in 1932. Surfacing on exercise, the hangar doors were opened too soon, allowing water to flood into the hull and send her to the bottom.

Moving to the South Devon coastline for Chapter Six, I have chosen the classic and seemingly delicate 1,382-ton schooner-rigged steamer *Bretagne* (1903), which was lost by collision in 1918. Its fine and distinctive lines are a complete contrast to the second Devon wreck I have chosen, for Chapter Five, the imposing and robust 3,616-ton SS *Maine*, which was torpedoed and sunk by a U-boat in 1917.

Chapter Seven covers one of the most important types of shipping of the Second World War, the wreck of American Liberty ship *James Eagan Layne* which lies in Whitsand Bay, Cornwall. The vast fleets of Liberty ships built by the great American industrial powerhouse to mass transport war materials and troops across the Atlantic to the battlefields of Europe were a key factor in victory in Europe. Without the supplies and munitions they brought to Britain there would have been no D-Day and perhaps no Allied victory. Their importance is often not recognised, but should not be underestimated.

For Chapter Eight I have chosen the 520-foot-long, 9,500 gross tons P&O passenger and mail ship *Moldavia*. A beautiful and massive ship built in 1903, she became a well-known sight on the Australia run. The dark days of the First World War however saw her commissioned by the British Admiralty and converted into an armed merchant cruiser and latterly into a troopship. Despite the *Moldavia*'s speed, *UB-57* caught up with her on 23 May 1916 and sent her to the bottom, off Sussex. Her massive remains lie 26 miles offshore in 50 metres of water in an area renowned for regular underwater visibility of in excess of 20 metres. She is a fantastic wreck to dive but massive in size and in deep water far offshore – she is not a dive for the fainthearted. Teeming with fish life, sealife, portholes still in situ, and filled with artefacts, most divers will hanker after diving her during their career.

Chapter Four deals with the wreck of the SS *Kyarra*, another First World War loss off Dorset. She lies in 30-plus metres of water not far out of the popular and picturesque port of Swanage, which has become something of a diving Mecca – the *Kyarra* is another huge favourite for divers. Although largely collapsed she is a fascinating dive with much to see and appreciate. Ironically, she was sent to the bottom by *UB-57*, the same U-boat that had sunk the *Moldavia* just three days earlier.

The 520-foot-long, 13,405-ton Cunard liner *Alaunia I* is the focus of Chapter Nine. Built in 1913, she saw only a very short civilian life on a regular Atlantic crossing to Canada and America. She was soon involved in the war effort sailing in convoy across the Atlantic taking troops and war supplies to Britain. After involvement in troop carrying in 1915 to Bombay and then the ill-fated Gallipoli campaign, in 1916 she was sent back to the cold waters of the Atlantic to ferry more troops from Canada and America. On 19 September 1916 she struck a mine two miles off the Royal Sovereign Lightship, Sussex, and sank. Although she has had salvage work carried out to her, she was a massive ship and all her fitments that lie around reveal this. Her bow section is intact; it has rolled onto its port side and is a stunning glimpse back to the era of beautiful and majestic shipping.

Each wreck is unique, a tantalising glimpse of the many and different forms of vessels which have come to grief in English waters. I have deliberately chosen wrecks which are safely diveable on air and are within easy and practical reach of the mainland, and so are relevant to today's divers. Although I have been a technical diver since 1995, diving mainly on Trimix, I have deliberately not included any wrecks that fall exclusively within the technical diver's realm.

Additionally I have not included wrecks that lie so far offshore or in such a remote location as to make them only rarely dived. This book is intended as a practical and useful guide to the most popular wrecks in English waters. If the scope of this book had been wider, I would certainly have included the *Pilsudski*, a 526-foot-long, 14,294-ton Polish liner that sank in 1939 after striking a mine. It is Yorkshire's largest diveable wreck, but lies some 25 miles offshore. Diving it requires an expedition approach and consequently it does not receive the diver attention that such a monstrous leviathan should.

Likewise the 11,130-ton SS *Rotorua*, a relatively intact 484-foot-long triple-screw, three-deck liner would certainly qualify as one of England's greatest. However, she lies in 55msw with a least depth of 44msw. This therefore is a deep air dive. As a critic of deep air, with its associated dangers, to make the best of this wreck I would use a lean Trimix to reduce the equivalent air narcotic depth. Although on merit the *Rotorua* should be in this book, in view of its long-distance offshore coupled with its depth, this wreck is only for the advanced or technical diver and so reluctantly I have omitted it from the book.

Diving conditions in English waters differ significantly from the conditions we experience in Scotland, where I do most of my diving. In trying to set up the dives on the wrecks it soon became apparent that diving them in visibility sufficient to survey them was not possible until the end of May. The trips I had set up for May had to be cancelled because of poor underwater visibility of 1–2 metres throughout the whole of that month. The plankton bloom, the May Waters, was so severe that it made the diving pointless. The waters clear rapidly at the end of May, heralding the start of the main diving season in the Channel from June onwards throughout the summer months. In Scotland we are fortunate to be able to dive all year round in relatively good visibility particularly on the West Coast, Scapa Flow and the Moray Firth. Although we are affected by the plankton bloom, the effects are not as severe as they would appear to be in the English Channel.

In laying out this book I have followed the format which I used in my first book, *Dive Scapa Flow* (Mainstream Publishing, Edinburgh 1990) and which I then developed in my second book, *Dive Scotland's Greatest Wrecks* (Mainstream Publishing, Edinburgh 1993). For each chapter I have devoted the first half to a historical account of the construction of the ship and the information about its seagoing days that I have been able to piece together. The second half of the chapter then recounts the condition of the wreck as it lies on the seabed today, with vital diver information on depth and currents. Cutaway sketches showing greatest and least depths are valuable to the diver in planning the dives, how long to stay down, what air supplies to carry and any decompression profile. Finally, Rob Ward of Illusion Illustration Limited, with complete professionalism was able to create the haunting impressions of the wrecks on the seabed. It has been a pleasure to work with such a professional again.

I hope that this book will provide a flavour of the tremendous variety and quality of the wreck-diving around England's shores. It is intended to be both informative and interesting – and at the same time to provide hard diver-orientated information which will be useful in planning dives and trips.

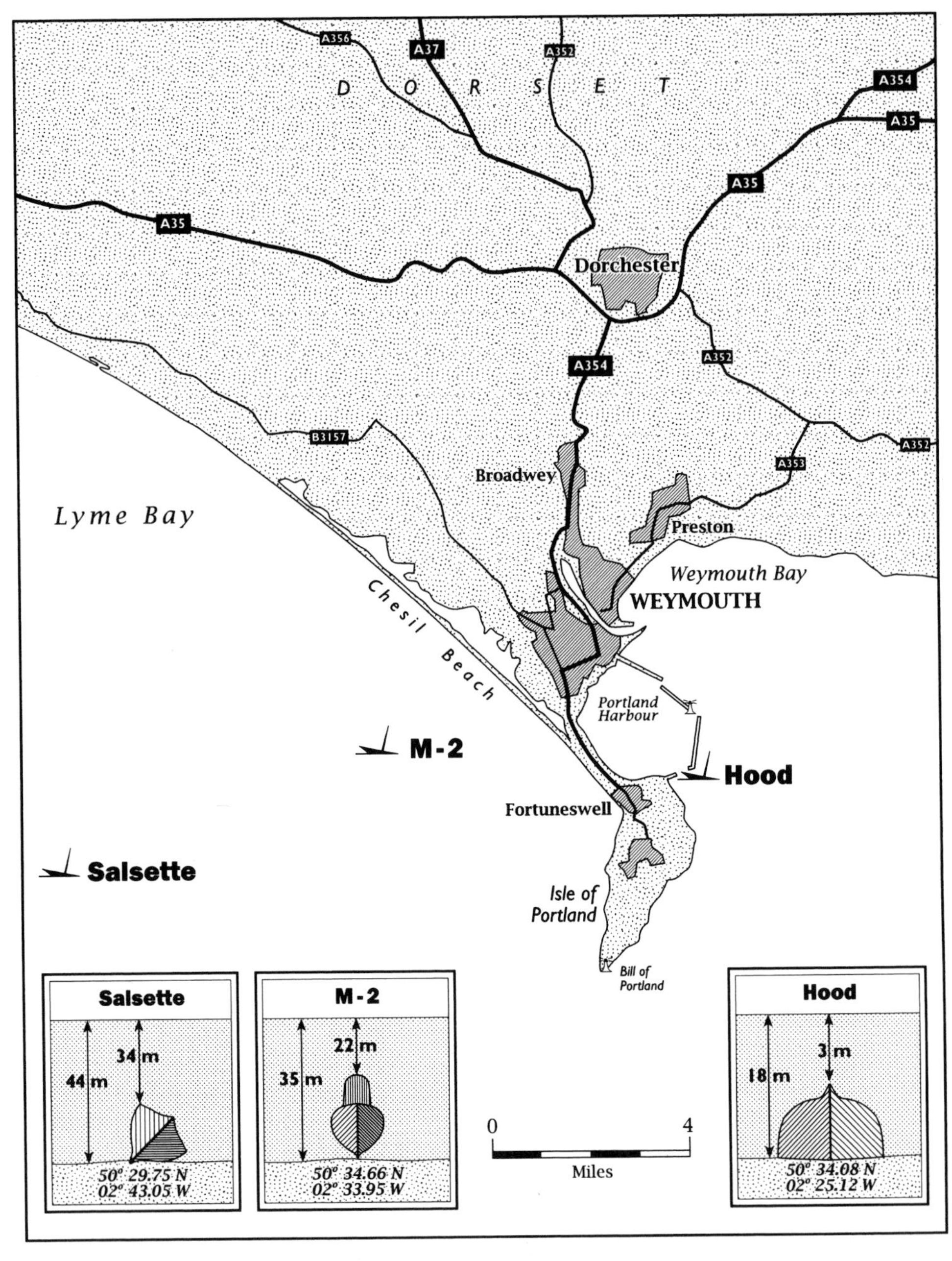
A356
A37
A352
D O R S E T
A354
A35
A35
A35
Dorchester
A354
A352
B3157
A352
A353
Broadwey
Preston
Lyme Bay
Weymouth Bay
WEYMOUTH
Chesil Beach
Portland Harbour
M-2
Hood
Fortuneswell
Salsette
Isle of Portland
Bill of Portland
Salsette
44 m
34 m
50° 29.75 N
02° 43.05 W
M-2
35 m
22 m
50° 34.66 N
02° 33.95 W
0
4
Miles
Hood
18 m
3 m
50° 34.08 N
02° 25.12 W

OPPOSITE:
LOCATION CHART
FOR WRECKS OF
THE *SALSETTE*,
HMS *HOOD* AND
HMS/M *M2*.

Chapter 1

THE *SALSETTE*, LYME BAY, DORSET

The 5,842-ton P&O express mail liner *Salsette* was regarded in her pre-war days as one of the most beautiful straight-stemmed steamships ever built. A sleek, elegant oceangoing liner, her hull was a uniform brilliant white, studded by two layers of some 600 portholes running her complete length. Her main mast and foremast were set at a rakish angle, matching her two yellow funnels.

The *Salsette* summed up the look of class and opulence that marked fine seagoing vessels of the era. Yet for all her elegance and speed, the dark clouds and grim deeds of the First World War overtook her and would consign her to the depths of the English Channel for eternity. Towards the end

THE BEAUTIFUL 5,842-TON P&O EXPRESS MAIL LINER *SALSETTE*
PHOTO COURTESY OF NATIONAL MARITIME MUSEUM, GREENWICH

of the war in 1917, she was attacked and torpedoed by *UB-40*. Fatally wounded, she sank into 44 metres of cold dark water, yet another testament to man's inhumanity to man. The *Salsette* is now justly regarded as one of England's greatest wrecks and draws large numbers of wreck divers to her each year.

In the era she was built, in 1908, steamships were beautifully crafted machines that boasted to the world the prowess of their mother nation. At the time it was customary to finish even small steamers with the finest of brass fitments. A prestigious flagship for the famous P&O line such as the *Salsette* would be particularly well furnished and trimmed. In the years following 1910, however, in the run up to the First World War, non-ferrous metals would be diverted into other more pressing uses, such as for the huge military build-up. From 1910 onwards, ships tended to have poorer-quality ferrous fitments and it is not uncommon, for example, in ships of that era to see ferrous portholes.

The *Salsette* was built in 1908 for the express mail service of the Peninsular and Oriental Steam Navigation Company, the famous P&O, by J. Caird and Co. in Greenock, Scotland, her official number being 127538. She was 440 feet long with a beam of 53 feet 2 inches and a draught of 19 feet 6 inches. Her gross tonnage was 5,842 tons, her net 2,392 tons. Her International Code Signal was H.M.R.J.

The *Salsette*'s twin bronze screws were powered by large quadruple-expansion engines with cylinders 28, 40, 57 and 82 inches in diameter and a stroke of 48 inches. Together these indicated 10,000hp and pushed her on to speeds of up to 20 knots. Her engines were fed by four double-ended and two single-ended boilers which worked at 215lb per square inch and were set up in two boiler-rooms.

In turn, each double-ended boiler had six furnaces and each single-ended boiler had three. The total heating surface was 23,151 square feet. The coal used to fire her boilers was loaded into her bunkers through coaling doors in the ship's side.

The *Salsette* was a sleek and beautiful ship built for the long passage to India – her name in fact was the name of a small island off Bombay. After her completion, in the summer of 1908, she ran her sea trials and was able to make 19.5 knots. Her hull was painted white and with her yellow funnels she cut a dashing figure. Her superstructure was initially painted the P&O standard light stone colour, but this soon gave way to a uniform white. After her sea trials, laden with guests of the owners, she made a delivery cruise down the Irish Sea and into the Bay of Biscay before passing on to Tilbury. There she was opened up to the public with an entry fee of one shilling, the proceeds of which went to the Seamen's Hospital.

From 8 to 31 August 1908, she made a pleasure cruise of the northern capitals visiting Amsterdam, the northern Norwegian city of Christiania (now known as

Oslo), Copenhagen, Kronstadt, Helsingfors and Kiel. Shortly after, from 8 September to 8 October, she made a second pleasure cruise to the Mediterranean visiting Gibraltar, Algiers, Corfu, Cattaro, Venice and Sicily before ending the cruise in Marseilles.

From Marseilles, in October 1908, she set out on her first working voyage to Bombay. Despite being held up for several hours in the Suez Canal she was able to break the company's Marseilles to Bombay record, setting a new record of 11 days and 21 hours.

The *Salsette* would also go on to break the longstanding Bombay to Aden record with a time of 3 days, 19 hours and 7 minutes. This entitled her to fly the golden cockerel emblem of the P&O on her jackstaff, the signal that she was the fastest vessel in the P&O fleet. She would later go on to win the Blue Ribband for the fastest crossing of the Atlantic.

Although the *Salsette* had been specially designed to carry passengers and mail and boasted a high standard of passenger accommodation, she was only able to carry a small amount of cargo in her 28-foot-deep holds. In the years leading up to the First World War she soon established herself as a famous and popular passenger steamer, with travellers to India vying to get a cabin aboard her.

With the assassination of Archduke Franz Ferdinand, heir to the Austro-Hungarian throne, and his wife in Sarejevo on 28 June 1914, the long-feared war that Europe had been gearing up towards in a great arms race exploded across the continent. The fatal shots were fired by Gavrilo Princip, a Bosnian student revolutionary, in support of the ideal of the separation of Bosnia–Herzegovina from the Austria–Hungary Habsburg empire and its union with Serbia, the inhabitants of which were ethnic fellows of the majority of Bosnia's population. Deep ethnic scars in this area have lasted for centuries and of course sparked the trouble there in more recent times.

The murders at Sarajevo led Austria–Hungary to take its strongest stand yet against Serbia, which was seen as the culprit in the agitation which threatened the stability of Europe. Austria–Hungary issued an ultimatum to Serbia – which was not complied with. This failure or refusal led to Austro-Hungary declaring war on Serbia, with German persuasion.

Russia feared that Austro–German power in the Balkans would threaten Constantinople and its main trade route from the Black Sea. Accordingly, Russia ordered a general mobilisation for war. This act resulted in Germany ordering a mobilisation for war the following day. Germany then issued a demand to Russia that she demobilise – but Russia declined to do so. German war plans had been formulated in advance and aimed for rapid knock-out blows and fierce aggression. In keeping with this, Russia's failure to demobilise resulted in Germany declaring war.

Under the Schlieffen Plan, German mobilisation demanded concentration of forces first against France, to neutralise it before concentrating on Russia. She knew that if Russia were attacked France would enter the war. German military planners also knew that they could not win a long war on two fronts against both France and Russia. Accordingly, with barely any excuse, two days after declaring war on Russia, on 3 August 1914, Germany declared war on France.

Germany then demanded that Belgium allow its armies free passage through Belgium to attack France but Belgium refused. Germany then invaded Belgium on 4 August. Britain, a bystander so far, had given a guarantee of Belgium's neutrality and so to honour that commitment, Britain declared war on Germany on 4 August 1914. The dogs of the greatest war the world had seen had been set loose.

Whilst these momentous events were unfolding across Europe the *Salsette* was at first untouched by the conflict. She was kept on her usual run until 1915. Then, because many of the regular mail ships had been requisitioned for Admiralty work, the *Salsette* was ordered back to Britain and put on the London to Bombay mail service. By that time the U-boat threat was fully appreciated but it was thought that the *Salsette*'s great speed of 20 knots would make her able to outrun any enemy U-boat. The fastest U-boats, travelling underwater, could achieve speeds of only around 7 knots, and only some 13 knots running exposed on the surface.

On her first such voyage, when she was in Marseilles, the French authorities captured two spies. On being questioned, they admitted that they had given information on her sailing times to a U-boat that was lying in wait outside the port for her. The *Salsette* delayed her departure for two days and was subsequently able to safely leave Marseilles unscathed to continue her journey to Bombay. For the return journey from Bombay she had not yet been fitted out with a defensive stern gun. So, in an effort to fool any enemy that might get her in its sights, the ship's carpenter made a dummy 4.7-inch defensive gun from wood and this was mounted at the stern. Off the Spanish coast, a U-boat approached her on the surface but was frightened off when the dummy gun was trained on it. The U-boat dived and made off as the *Salsette* sped past.

Safely back in London, a real 4.7-inch stern defensive gun was fitted, intended to fire on the enemy as the *Salsette* used her speed to escape any pursuer. Whilst the dummy gun had proved valuable, the real gun would never be used in anger.

On her next voyage, outward bound with mail and passengers for Bombay, the *Salsette* was stranded in the Gulf of Suez off Ras Abu Dorez. Her condensers became clogged and blocked with sand and she had to be pulled off by the French cruiser *Montcalm*. The British cruisers *Fox* and *Proserpine* stood by to assist and the operation was successfully completed without any significant damage being suffered by the *Salsette*.

On her return from Bombay to London the *Salsette* was then put into service travelling to Australia via Bombay and Colombo. In 1916–17 she made two round voyages to Sydney. She then returned to the shuttle service for a short time before sailing in July 1917 from London with a large consignment of money to pay troops in Egypt before heading on to Sydney.

However, in the same month, sheer bad luck brought her close to a 260-ton U-boat, *UB-40*. *UB-40* was a small and slow U-boat, part of the Flanders Flotilla based in Zeebruge and Bruges. She could only manage 9 knots on the surface and 5–6 knots submerged. She couldn't chase her prey – she would wait until it fell into her path.

UB-40 was commanded by Oberleutnant zur See Howaldt, one of Germany's ace submariners and one of the few who would survive the war, when the average life span of a U-boat captain was 60 days. By the end of the war, the Flanders Flotilla was losing one U-boat a week.

In the middle of July 1917 Howaldt took *UB-40* from its base and slipped through the British barrage of nets and mines in the Channel. On 15 July he surfaced off the Sussex coast and sank a small group of English fishing boats with a boarding party, a practice he employed when dealing with sailing vessels. To save expending a valuable torpedo on small prey he would use *UB-40*'s gun or a bomb to sink the vessel after allowing the crew to abandon ship. With the British use of Q-ships, seemingly innocuous small vessels with hidden guns manned by crack Royal Navy gunners, this had become an increasingly dangerous practice.

After this action *UB-40* proceeded to Lyme Bay, where, not seeing any targets, Howaldt prepared to wait until shipping came his way. It turned out to be a long wait of four days before, on 20 July, the tell-tale black smoke of the coal-fired engines of a big ship approaching from the east got the crew to action stations. Howaldt gave the order to dive. *UB-40* quickly slipped beneath the waves to periscope depth. Howaldt then put the boat's engines ahead and headed towards the oncoming vessels – one of which was the *Salsette*.

Under the command of Captain A.B. Armitage, RNR, the *Salsette* had anchored in the Downs the evening before, 19 July at 7 p.m. At 10.30 p.m. Captain Armitage had received his orders to proceed to Bombay. As the *Salsette* started off on her long journey she approached the Shambles Lightship. Here, the course she was to take was signalled to her by a patrol vessel. The *Salsette* started to work up speed and commenced zig-zagging following Admiralty instructions.

By noon the following day, 20 July, the *Salsette* was in Lyme Bay still moving at speed and zig-zagging. It was on one of these turns that she passed right across the firing position that Howaldt in *UB-40* had adopted. At just after 12.01 p.m, Howaldt gave the order to fire from close range.

Aboard the *Salsette* the tell-tale trace of *UB-40*'s torpedo was spotted by her

Chief Officer who was on the monkey-bridge taking bearings. He shouted out 'Hard a-starboard'. Captain Armitage heard the commotion and rushed out from the chart room where he had been plotting the ship's next course alteration, and repeated the order.

The ship had been given no time to answer the helm. There was a huge explosion on her starboard side that threw Captain Armitage to the ground. A column of water, the classic sign of a torpedo strike, exploded upwards to hang suspended in the air before crashing back down onto the decks.

Captain Armitage picked himself up and, reaching the engine-room, telegraphed 'Stop'. He realised already that his ship was mortally wounded. She felt dead in the water and it seemed that she was collapsing inwards like a deck of cards. He gave the order 'Abandon ship and engine-room'.

The torpedo from *UB-40* had exploded on the starboard side of the *Salsette* in the engine-room area, causing a scene of mayhem there as pieces of machinery and coal were thrown around. Fourteen Indian firemen employed to feed coal to the boilers died immediately as the hull of the ship was rent open allowing tons of sea water to start flooding into the engine-room. Scalding steam sprayed from burst pipes and there would have been further explosions as the cold sea water came into contact with the boilers.

Despite all her watertight doors being shut and her main deck scuttles being fitted with deadlights that would prevent water getting into the ship, the damage to her hull was so catastrophic that nothing could prevent the onrush of water into her. Her fate was sealed.

The passengers had already had their lifeboat drill, particularly vital in wartime, and knew their places. As a result, the abandonment of the ship took place very speedily and within five minutes the lifeboats were full, lowered and pulling away from the ship.

Captain Armitage and a few officers stayed behind along with lifeboat No. 3 and systematically went about specific tasks to ensure that no secret or militarily sensitive documents and papers were left aboard. After all, the ship might remain afloat long enough to be boarded and searched by the U-boat crew. There was also a chance that documents could float free from the sinking ship and end up in enemy hands. Accordingly, the ship's papers were placed in a weighted bag and dropped overboard.

The captain ordered the radio operator to continuously send a message that the *Salsette* was under submarine attack – until he was forced by the rising sea to leave the radio room for his own safety. Once the ship had been cleansed of all important documents the captain and his remaining crew boarded lifeboat No. 3 and rowed away from *Salsette*.

The water flooding into her hull caused the *Salsette* to heel progressively further to her port side. Within 28 minutes from the torpedo strike, at about 12.30 p.m., the *Salsette* slipped beneath the waves and the waters closed over her. She then plunged down through 44 metres of cold, dark sea water before impacting onto the silty seabed sending up billowing clouds of silt. Gradually the silt settled, covering the wreck with a fine layer. Another casualty of man's inhumanity to man had found its final resting place in the silent depths on the bottom of the sea.

After confirming his kill Oberleutnant Howaldt took *UB-40* down into the depths and made to leave the scene of the sinking. Soon however, Royal Navy destroyers, alerted by the emergency sub-attack broadcast, arrived on the scene and started a pattern of depth charging. Huge, crumping explosions shook the depths followed by secondary brilliant white eruptions of sea water.

The destroyers searched extensively for the U-boat and Howaldt was forced to take *UB-40* down to the seabed and lie silent, hoping that his pursuers would pass by. On one run however, depth charges exploded so close to *UB-40* that the shockwave started a minor leak in the engine-room.

After lying silently on the bottom for an hour and hearing the sounds of the British activity fading into the distance, Howaldt judged that all was clear and cautiously took *UB-40* up to periscope depth. Peering through the periscope, Howaldt could make out the British destroyers in the distance continuing their depth-charging patterns. Meanwhile other vessels were picking up the *Salsette*'s survivors in the lifeboats. The now-empty lifeboats themselves were taken in tow in line astern towards Weymouth.

As Howaldt scanned the horizon from his periscope he saw a small steamship with a stern defensive gun approaching his position. A lesser man, having just survived intense British depth-charging may have let this vessel pass by and made good his escape. However Howaldt was a tenacious captain and he immediately ordered his crew to prepare to attack this vessel and to calculate his attacking run.

The new prey for *UB-40* was the *L.H. Carl*, a 1,916-ton British steamship en route from Barry to Rouen. Howaldt fired again with great accuracy. His torpedo struck the *L.H. Carl*, fatally wounding her and sending her to the bottom very quickly with the loss of two members of crew. This further attack alerted the British destroyers to *UB-40*'s whereabouts and they charged over to the scene of the fresh attack and started a further series of heavy depth-charging runs.

Skilfully, Howaldt was able to evade these attempts as well and head back for Zeebruge, which he would reach five days later on 25 July. He docked *UB-40* safely in its pen in the early hours before dawn.

Once the *Salsette*'s survivors had arrived at Weymouth the Royal Navy Chief Examination Officer arranged hotel accommodation for the passengers and the crew were put up in the Sailor's Home. At 6.45 p.m. that evening, 20 July 1917,

Captain Armitage went to Weymouth General Post Office and sent a telegram to the P&O offices in London:

> Destroyed by enemy. Nine firemen five coal-trimmers killed. All passengers and remainder of ship's company saved and uninjured. Ship sank in 28 minutes, boats away in 5 minutes. What is to be done with boats. Admiralty instructions carried out. Zig-zag at time. No warning. Making arrangements for passengers and crew to proceed London. Armitage.

Soon after the *Salsette*'s sinking Howaldt was promoted to Kapitänleutnant and given command of one of the latest U-boats, *UB-107*, a 640-ton vessel. This was a far superior U-boat to *UB-40*, with four bow tubes and one stern tube – she could also manage 14 knots on the surface compared to *UB-40*'s top speed of just over 9 knots. In *UB-107* Howaldt would go on to score many more successes against Allied shipping over the course of the coming year. In July 1918 he took some leave and Kapitänleutnant Von Prittwitz und Gaffron took over in command. On that very first trip under new command, on 27 July 1918, *UB-107* was trapped off Scarborough and successfully depth-charged by a group of armed trawlers.

One month before the Armistice of November 1918 halted the fighting, Flanders fell to the Allies. Howaldt's first U-boat, *UB-40*, was blown up by the Germans in Bruges on 2 October 1918 as the U-boat base was evacuated.

Today the wreck of the once-beautiful *Salsette* is justly acclaimed as one of the finest wrecks in English waters and draws large numbers of divers to her each year. She lies some 11.5 nautical miles west of Portland Bill at Position 50 29.748 N, 002 43.049 W in 44 metres of sea water (msw). Given her distance offshore she makes an enjoyable hard boat dive with hard boats from Portland taking about 40 minutes to an hour to get out to the site.

The *Salsette* lies resting on her port side in an average depth, excluding the bow and stern scours, of 44msw. The least depth to her uppermost starboard rail is an average 34msw. Although all of her superstructure has long since rotted away, the hull remains relatively intact and retains its ship shape despite the ravages of nearly 90 years lying at the bottom of the Channel. The fine lines of its once meticulously cleaned and polished wooden decking can still be made out.

To add to the attraction of this fabled wreck the underwater visibility in this area of the Channel is often, in the summer months, an average of 10–20 metres. This glorious visibility allows divers to see a lot of the ship at any one time and

DIVE DETAILS FOR THE *SALSETTE*

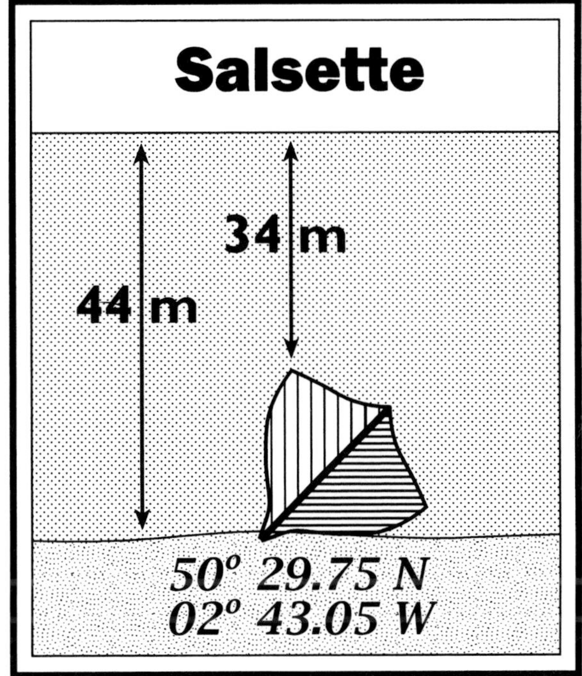

helps them gain an appreciative understanding of being able to dive this relic from a bygone age of steam.

At the very bow divers can make out the classic straight stem so reminiscent of steamers of her era. Moving underneath the overhanging portside of the majestic bow, the port-side anchor can be found still sitting snugly in its hawse pipe. A tidal scour around the bow section has excavated the seabed here down to a depth of 46msw. The higher starboard-side anchor is also still securely held in its hawse pipe. The anchor chains run back through the hull onto the now almost vertical deck to the huge anchor winch. From here they descend beneath the deck to the chain locker. At either side of the bow, mooring bollards and cleats are dotted about.

On the deck, between the anchor chains, stands a small crane which was used for manoeuvring the anchors and which rises to 32msw, the shallowest point of the wreck. If

THE HAUNTING REMAINS OF THE WRECK OF THE *SALSETTE* LIE AT THE BOTTOM OF LYME BAY. © ROD MACDONALD 2003

an anchor was lost the spare anchor could be winched over the side and connected up using this crane. Slightly aft of this, at either side of the deck stand steam-driven capstans that worked the cargo cranes and derricks.

The large foremast has broken off and fallen to the seabed below. Aft of its stump, originally situated one on either side of the deck, are cargo cranes set on pivoting bases and used for loading and unloading the foredeck holds. Both cranes are collapsing downwards from their mountings.

Aft of the foremast large hatches and openings are found. These allowed access to the foredeck holds. Just aft of these, the remains of the once-imposing bridge superstructure rise out of the gloom. The thin steel and wood of the walls of this deckhouse were not constructed with decades of immersion in sea water in mind. They have in the main all rotted away leaving very little of the superstructure visible other than some structural girders and beams in places.

Moving further aft of the bridge area itself, the *Salsette*'s two funnels have collapsed and crumpled to the seabed. Like the superstructure, these towering funnels had to be constructed of lightweight materials to avoid too much weight high up. The cavernous flues that led from the funnels to the engine-room have become filled with debris. Around this area once stood a forest of forced draught ventilator funnels with their open bell ends. These have in the main now also collapsed to the seabed leaving only their stumps and black openings below decks.

The torpedo from *UB-40* struck the *Salsette* on the starboard side of the engine-room. Beneath the waterline on the starboard side here the large hole left by the fatal explosion is visible. It is possible to penetrate the engine-room from an opening on the main deck and to exit the hull through the torpedo damage on the starboard side of the hull.

Once beyond the areas above the boiler-room, engine-room and funnels, the base of the main mast is found – the mast itself long ago collapsed to the seabed. Two decks of passenger cabins here line the sides of the ship and offer much opportunity for penetration work by suitably experienced and qualified divers.

Moving from here further aft, the yawning chasm of her after deck holds seems to open up the hull right down to her bottom. On the uppermost starboard side, the hull here is now collapsing in and starting to lose its ship shape. The same cargo cranes on pivoting bases as were found at the foredeck holds are also found around the stern holds, again having fallen from their mounts.

At the very stern the ship regains its shape again. Although the *Salsette* was a twin-screw ship, the uppermost starboard side propeller has been salvaged. The 4.7-inch defensive gun, never fired in anger, still remains in situ here.

At 440 feet long, it is just possible for divers to make the grand tour of her remains in one dive, perhaps finding areas that they would like to return to on another dive to explore in detail. Varying between 34 and 44msw, the *Salsette* is at a depth where divers working hard to fin her length will quickly eat into their air supplies. On the dives that I did to survey the wreck, I used an underwater scooter or Diver Propulsion Vehicle (DPV), which meant that we were able to cover the whole wreck with ease without having to work hard finning. The more relaxed you are underwater the less air you will consume.

The *Salsette* can be dived quite easily on air although at these depths all divers will be suffering the effects of a diving condition known as *nitrogen narcosis*. The deeper you dive the more the increasing weight of water above you tries to compress your air spaces such as your lungs and sinal cavities. To avoid your lungs being collapsed inwards by the increasing water pressure, a diver's aqualung feeds into his lungs as he breathes, air at an increasing pressure which matches exactly the water pressure outwith his body. With the air pressure in a diver's lungs at the same pressure as the water pressure surrounding him the diver is safe from harm.

If it were not so, and the water pressure was greater than the pressure in his lungs, he would be in serious danger.

The greater pressures of air being fed into a diver's lungs by his aqualung means that far larger concentrations of air are going into his lungs compared to the surface. A gas called nitrogen makes up 79 per cent of air. On the surface, nitrogen passes in and out of our body without affecting us in any way. By the time a diver is down at a depth of 40 metres, the water pressure around him is five times the air pressure we experience on the surface, atmospheric pressure. To maintain the pressure equilibrium between lungs and the water outside, a diver's aqualung or breathing regulator feeds air from his tank into his lungs at five times atmospheric pressure. Five times as much air is therefore passing into the diver's body – and this means that five times as much nitrogen is also passing into his body.

Although largely inert on the surface, the increasing amounts of nitrogen have a narcotic effect on a diver – the so-called 'raptures of the depths'. Divers on the *Salsette* diving on compressed air will all be suffering the effects of *nitrogen narcosis*. The 'narcs' affect different people in different ways, depending on experience and ability. To enable us to work more efficiently underwater surveying this wreck, we wanted to reduce the debilitating effects of *nitrogen narcosis*. Therefore, on our *Salsette* dives, Steve Collard and I used a lean trimix of oxygen (19 per cent), helium (34 per cent) and nitrogen. The normal 79 per cent of nitrogen was reduced by the 34 per cent helium to a less damaging 47 per cent. Helium is inert and has no narcotic effect on the human body. In real terms, this meant that although I was diving at a depth of 45msw, by getting rid of a large percentage of the narcotic nitrogen, the narcotic effect on my body from that reduced percentage of nitrogen gave me an equivalent narcotic depth of 23 metres. In other words, although I was diving at 45 metres, my body was absorbing the nitrogen that I would take in if I were diving on air at only 23 metres. At that depth on air, a diver is barely affected by *nitrogen narcosis*. As a result, my head was clear and not muddied by the effects of narcosis. On our ascent we changed over to smaller tanks slung beneath our arms that contained a different gas, Nitrox 50, for decompression from a depth of 20msw to the surface. This gas, a mix of 50 per cent oxygen and 50 per cent nitrogen speeds up the process of getting rid of the gas breathed at depth from the body.

The *Salsette* is a haunting and moving wreck. Its size is dominating and it is sometimes difficult to work out exactly where on the wreck you are at first. There is so much to see and take in wherever you are on the wreck, from the majestic bows to the characteristic stern. In addition, large schools of fish hang like curtains across some parts of the wreck slowly moving, shimmering and

THE BEACH SLIP AT PORTLAND HARBOUR IS SUITABLE FOR LAUNCHING RIGID INFLATABLE BOATS (RIBS). PHOTO: AUTHOR'S COLLECTION

changing with the current. This once-famous vessel of a still-famous shipping line exerts a draw that has proved irresistible for countless divers. She is certainly one of the classic English wreck dives.

Essential Information

BOAT LAUNCH SITE: For RIBs, slips are available at Weymouth, Portland, West Bay and Lyme Regis. Harbour and launch fees payable.

HARD BOAT DIVING: In Portland – Breakwater Diving Centre (01305) 860269, The Scuba Centre (01305 826666, Underwater Expolrers (01305) 824555, Portland Oceaneering Ltd (01305) 860402, Fathom & Blues (01305) 826789. In Weymouth – *Channel Chieftain* (01305) 787155, *Skin Deep* (01305) 782556, Old Harbour Dive Centre (01305) 760888, *Kyarratoo* (07774) 993326, *Wey Chieftain*, *Dive Time*, *Diver City*.

TIDAL CONDITIONS: Dive at slack water.

VISIBILITY: Winter 2–3 metres. June through summer, 10–20 metres.

MAXIMUM DEPTH: 46 metres in bow and stern scours. General depth 44 metres.

LEAST DEPTH: 34msw to starboard rail.

COASTGUARD: Portland and Weymouth Coastguard (01305) 760439.

RECOMPRESSION FACILITIES: Poole Hyperbaric Hotline (01426) 316636, (03367) 771883. Institute of Naval Medicine Gosport Hotline (07831) 151523.

AIR SUPPLIES: In Portland – Breakwater Diving Centre (01305) 860269, Fathom & Blues, The Scuba Centre, Underwater Explorers, Portland Oceaneeering Ltd (tel. nos. above).

HYDROGRAPHIC CHART: Berry Head to Bill of Portland, No. 315.

POSITION: Lat 50 29.748 N, Long 002 43.049 W.

DIVER LEVEL: Given the depth and distance offshore this wreck is for the experienced diver only. No-stop diving is not practical on the deeper sections of this wreck. Decompression stops will be required dependent on bottom times.

Chapter 2

HMS *Hood*, Portland Harbour, Dorset

The British pre-dreadnought battleship HMS *Hood* was commissioned in 1889, being the eighth battleship provided for by the Naval Defence Act of March 1889. At the time of her launch at Chatham two years later, in 1891, she was a state-of-the-art vehicle of war, heavily armed and heavily armoured. She symbolised the power and might of the Royal Navy and boasted to the world of the prowess of the nation that created her. Yet, within the short space of 15 years, there would be a quantum leap forward in battleship

THE BRITISH PRE-DREADNOUGHT BATTLESHIP, HMS *HOOD*.
PHOTO COURTESY OF THE NATIONAL MARITIME MUSEUM, GREENWICH

design that would render her obsolete and unfit to fight in the coming Great War of 1914–18.

At the time of her launch she was seen as a colossal and powerful fighting machine, weighing in at 14,150 tons. She was 410 feet in length with a beam of 75 feet and draught of 27.5 feet. She boasted four 13.5-inch guns as her main armament, set in two twin heavily armoured turrets, one forward and one aft.

Her secondary armament consisted mainly of ten independently fired powerful 6-inch guns set in single turrets ranged along either side of the ship. These rapid-firing smaller guns were designed for use against fast enemy surface vessels trying to close to attack *Hood* at its most vulnerable point, broadside on.

Although HMS *Hood* was the state of the art in naval warfare at the time of her launch, ship development, both civilian and military, was leaping forward. HMS *Hood* was unknowingly entering service with the Royal Navy shortly before what was to be the single greatest change in warship evolution – the development of a new breed of warship, the dreadnought.

The design and thinking behind a new British battleship, HMS *Dreadnought* launched in 1906 was so revolutionary that it would give its name to this new class of supreme warship. Almost overnight, the new dreadnoughts would render all the pre-dreadnoughts afloat obsolete. Such was the effect of the development of the dreadnoughts that, just over ten years after her 1893 commission into the Royal Navy, *Hood* and her sister *Royal Sovereign* (R class) battleships had become relics of a bygone era, obsolete to the extent that these once all-powerful vessels would have no role to play in the looming conflict of the First World War, the greatest conflict the world had ever seen.

In the closing years of the nineteenth century, Britain and Germany became locked in an arms race – a race that would lead to the eventual creation of the dreadnought and to the end of the sea lives of many pre-dreadnoughts, such as HMS *Hood*. The Royal Navy had for centuries gauged its strength by the famous 'two-power standard'. The philosophy behind this standard was that the Royal Navy must always be equal in strength to the combined seapower of the second- and third-largest navies in the world.

At the end of the nineteenth century Kaiser Wilhelm II and the then Captain Alfred von Tirpitz dreamed of ending Britain's naval supremacy and of winning control of the seas. Together they masterminded a huge German naval arms build-up. This caused much concern to the British Admiralty, who had to match it if they were to continue to adhere to their enshrined two-power standard. So began a momentous arms race as both sides geared up for a war that seemed increasingly unavoidable.

In 1906, Britain got the breakthrough it needed with the revolutionary construction of HMS *Dreadnought*. She was so far ahead of her time that she gave her name to this new breed of ship. The new dreadnoughts were about 10 per cent bigger than their predecessors such as HMS *Hood* and at £1.75 million (in 1905), much more expensive. The dreadnoughts were faster and had thicker armour and greater fire-power than the pre-dreadnoughts such as *Hood.* Each had ten 12-inch guns set in five twin turrets, compared to *Hood*'s four 13.5-inch guns in two twin turrets. Dreadnought guns were able to hurl 850lb shells for 18,500 yards – *Hood* had a firing range of less than 16,000 yards.

Initially, three of the dreadnought's five twin gun turrets were centred on the middle line of the vessel with a further turret set either side amidships. The leap in scale and fighting power that the dreadnought brought was momentous and it helps to give an idea of that leap if the fighting characteristics of the two breeds are compared directly:

- The dreadnought could fire a broadside of *eight* shells to either side, whilst the pre-dreadnoughts fired a broadside of *four* shells.
- The dreadnought could fire *six* shells ahead. The pre-dreadnought could only fire *two* shells ahead.

An increase in fire-power and indeed protective armour was only half the story. In yet another quantum leap in battleship

THE PRE-DREADNOUGHT HMS *HOOD* IN HER EARLY LIVERY.
PHOTO COURTESY OF THE NATIONAL MARITIME MUSEUM, GREENWICH

design, for the first time all eight guns in a broadside, which on pre-dreadnoughts such as *Hood* were fired independently, could now be aimed and fired in unison by one gunnery officer. One dreadnought could thus match two pre-dreadnoughts for fire-power at long range and three pre-dreadnoughts when firing ahead.

HMS *Hood* was built at the Chatham Dockyard, one of the eight Royal Sovereign R Class battleships on which construction started in 1889 and 1890. The others in the class were *Royal Sovereign* herself, *Emperor of India*, *Ramillies*, *Repulse*, *Resolution*, *Revenge* and *Royal Oak*.

The Royal Sovereign R class vessels were all fitted out with cylindrical boilers which fired two sets of Humphreys triple-expansion engines and developed 13,000ihp, enough to drive her twin screws to achieve 17.5 knots. The fastest of the class, *Royal Oak* could achieve 18.27 knots. The new breed of dreadnoughts that would follow in the run-up to the First World War could achieve a much faster speed of 23 knots. Thus *Hood* and her pre-dreadnought sister ships were doomed to become slow ships, unable to keep up with the newer dreadnoughts in the Fleet.

Hood was protected by an 18-inch-thick main armour belt with 4 inches of hard-faced steel above as protection against secondary weapons. Her deck armour was 3 inches thick and her barbettes (the armoured shafts descending from her main gun turrets) were 17 inches thick. In addition to her four 13.5-inch guns, set side by side in two turrets, *Hood* boasted ten 6-inch casemate guns. These were set in single mounts along either side of the main midships section of superstructure. Four of the casemates had 6-inch-thick armoured protection. The other six had upper deck light shields only, although they were given 6-inch armoured casemate protection in 1902–4.

Hood was also armed with 16 quick-firing 6-pounders, 12 quick-firing 3-pounders and 4 MGs. The 6-pounders were set in single mounts in elevated positions around the vessel. Some were set in the large circular platforms on the main mast and foremast accessed by climbing up the masts on steel ladder rungs. Others were set in the smaller searchlight and spotting platforms higher still up the masts. Six-pounders were also mounted on top of the main 13.5-inch gun turrets and along the deck level above.

Lastly she was fitted out with seven 18-inch torpedo tubes, of which two were submerged below the water line. Along either side were mounted diagonal booms that would swing outwards to deploy anti-torpedo netting. HMS *Hood* carried a ship's complement of 712 officers and men.

After her commission in 1893 HMS *Hood* quickly gained a reputation as a good-looking battleship, but a very poor seagoing vessel. She was weighed down greatly by the heavily armoured turrets for her twin 13.5-inch main guns which the First Sea Lord, Sir Arthur Hood, had insisted were latterly installed. This extra weight had lowered her freeboard and resulted in her needing very calm conditions if she were to make any speed at all. In heavier seas her bow dipped and bashed into the waves, resulting in a lot of water and spray sweeping the ship and making effective gunnery impossible. She was ill suited to the North Sea and Atlantic waters and so not long after her completion she was sent to the quieter waters of the Mediterranean, where she stayed on duty for nine years.

During the years 1905 to 1910, coinciding with the development and deployment of HMS *Dreadnought* and her class of superior battleships, the Royal Sovereign R Class battleships were taken out of the frontline fleet and put on reserve duties, *Hood* being one of the first of her class to do so in 1905. Thereafter she was transferred to Portland as a target for torpedo practices and her heavy guns were taken out. Ironically, for all the planning and design work that had gone into her, for all the years of toil and hard work in the dockyards by thousands of dockyard workers building her up and for all the years of service and meticulous maintenance needed to keep her afloat, *Hood* had never fired her guns once in anger.

With the outbreak of the First World War most of the Royal Sovereign R Class battleships were sent for scrapping or used as gunnery targets. Only HMS *Revenge* got a brief respite when she was reactivated for the war in 1914 and used as a bombardment ship off the Belgian coast in 1914. Her guns were outdated and had a limited range compared to the newer vessels but her crew evolved a clever way of increasing the range of her main guns. Torpedo bulges had been fitted to her hull along both sides as a protection against torpedo strikes and mines. The crew would flood a torpedo bulge along one side of the hull with sea water. This caused the ship to list over to that side and consequently lifted the other side of the ship higher, increasing the elevation of her guns and thus achieving a greater striking distance.

When stocks of the old specification 13.5-inch shells for her main guns ran out, her guns were relined to 12-inch. This increased their effective range to 16,000 yards. She was renamed *Redoubtable* in 1915 to release her original name for a new battleship. Shortly thereafter, in the same year, she was deactivated and was latterly scrapped in 1919.

By November 1914, HMS *Hood* had come to the end of her useful sea career. In the rush to arm for war, the Admiralty could not afford to have precious crews and facilities tied up in keeping a ship afloat that had only a very limited potential use. The development of effective submarines was comparatively recent, but the potential German submarine threat was understood and feared. The Admiralty were aware that Germany had embarked on an intensive submarine construction programme earlier that year which would double the number of their U-boats by the end of 1914.

HMS *Hood* was earmarked to end her days by being scuttled as a blockship across the southern entrance to Portland harbour. The Admiralty wanted to seal this entrance to stop U-boats penetrating into the harbour itself or indeed from lurking outside the harbour entrance and firing torpedoes into the harbour at the anchored Channel Fleet.

On 4 November 1914 *Hood* was towed into the chosen defensive position. She was to be sunk at slack water to ensure she ended up correctly sealing the entrance. Her seacocks were opened, the idea being to allow her to sink gracefully and proudly in an upright position. Her pace of sinking however turned out to be too slow and the tide soon turned – before the scuttling was completed. Soon, the strong tide was pulling her out of position. Explosives were hurriedly used to blow a hole in her side, but once she was blown open, huge volumes of water rushed into her. Battleships were renowned for their instability once flooded and it was common to find them turning turtle. *Hood* was no exception – the inrushing waters soon caused her to roll to her port side and then turn upside down and sink quickly to the seabed. Although things had not gone quite to plan, with a depth of just 2 metres over her upturned keel she very effectively eliminated any clandestine entry into the harbour, or indeed any torpedo being fired at ships inside the harbour. Nearly 90 years later *Hood* still rests in position at the entrance, still blocking it to navigation for any craft bigger than small RIBs and hard boats.

Today HMS *Hood* lies upside down in 15–18 metres of water, her bows pointing to the east, just outside the southern entrance to Portland harbour. The whale back of her broad kelp-covered keel still rises up to just a few metres from the surface. Her shallow depth means that she is a wreck suitable for the novice diver to practice wreck-diving drills on. For the more experienced and suitably trained diver, *Hood* offers the possibility of some serious penetration work into the bowels of this once-powerful leviathan.

ABOVE: THE COLOSSAL REMAINS OF THE BRITISH PRE-DREADNOUGHT BATTLESHIP HMS *HOOD* STILL BLOCK THE SOUTHERN ENTRANCE TO PORTLAND HARBOUR.

© ROD MACDONALD 2003

BELOW: THE TWO PIERS OF THE SOUTHERN ENTRANCE TO PORTLAND HARBOUR. THE SMALL BUOY IS ATTACHED TO THE STERN OF HMS *HOOD*. NOTE THE CABLE STRUNG ACROSS THE ENTRANCE TO PREVENT SHIPPING ATTEMPTING TO NAVIGATE THIS CHANNEL.

THE PONTOON AT PORTLAND HARBOUR FROM WHERE LOCAL HARD BOATS AND RIBS REGULARLY DEPART FOR HMS *HOOD*. PHOTO: AUTHOR'S COLLECTION

THE SOUTHERNMOST PIER AT PORTLAND HARBOUR. THE SMALL BUOY TO THE LEFT IS ATTACHED TO THE STERN OF THE WRECK AND IS THE STARTING POINT FOR MOST DIVES ON *HOOD*'S REMAINS. PHOTO: AUTHOR'S COLLECTION

HMS *Hood* can be dived from either RIBs or hard boats. Alternatively her remains can be shore-dived by descending down the large jumble of concrete blocks, the foundation for the breakwater. Here, there is usually a small buoy out of the prevailing current. From here a guide rope leads through the jumble of blocks to a post at seabed level on the outermost port-side stern section of the wreck.

Here, at the stern, the large rudder still stands, defying the endless, remorselessly changing current and dwarfing divers with its sheer size. The propeller shafts project from the hull alongside, the propellers themselves having been removed before her scuttling.

Moving forward and dropping down towards the seabed, some large sections of plating have fallen free from the side of the ship, allowing easy access to the innards of the vessel. Inside, there are large pieces of once floor-mounted machinery now suspended from above. Great care should be taken here as from time to time, with the natural degradation of the wreck, some collapsing occurs and there is always the potential for these heavy parts to fall downwards.

Before her scuttling the main 13.5-inch guns of the *Hood* had been removed but her secondary 6-inch casemate gun positions ranged along either side of her midship's superstructure were left in situ. After almost 90 years sitting on the bottom, with the colossal weight of the *Hood* driving downwards, this superstructure is now partly buried in the seabed which rises up to cover the tops of the upside-down 6-inch casemate turrets. The sheer, angular lines of the upturned superstructure can easily be seen, studded with portholes which give divers a glimpse into the pitch blackness of her interior. Crumpled and torn plating lies scattered on the seabed.

Hood had three 6-inch casemate guns set in integral turrets on either side of this superstructure. As divers move forward from the stern area, the upturned bottom of the aftmost 6-inch casemate gun turret looms into view beneath them, projecting outwards from the sheer armoured plating of the superstructure.

Above, at the bulwark rail, an unusual fixed grating walkway runs the whole length of the superstructure and projects outwards from the side of the hull. To minimise danger from plunging fire the superstructure was designed almost flush with the side of the ship. This walkway allowed crew to quickly move from the forward section of the ship to the after section without having to go through the huge superstructure. The walkway is broken in places where the large booms used to deploy her anti-torpedo netting hang down.

Further forward the base of the smaller middle casemate gun turret can be found, slightly lower than the two larger casemate turrets either side of it. In between these three main casemate turrets are recessed small openings for *Hood*'s smaller weaponry. Two large black doors are set in this superstructure, one to the forward section and one to the rear, allowing divers a glimpse into the dark interior. Green shafts of light can be seen in places, penetrating inwards to lift the veil of darkness hiding the innards of her hull. Vertical rows of ladder rungs are still fixed in place leading from the walkway down (but now up) to the original waterline and which allowed crews from tenders and pinnaces to board the ship.

Moving further forward, divers will find that the bow section forward of the superstructure stands off the seabed at first, allowing them to catch sight of the location of the 13.5-inch forward gun turret. The very bow itself, however, rests on the foundations for the eastmost harbour pier. Higher up on the hull at both ends of the superstructure there is evidence that the structural integrity of the hull is weakened. Fore and aft of the superstructure, plating has sprung off the hull and fallen to the seabed to reveal the ribs of her hull.

Hood's large superstructure was heavily armoured; it was, and remains, hugely strong. The ship rests upside down largely supported by this superstructure with the bow itself sitting on the shallower jumble of foundation blocks for the eastmost pier. The colossal weight of her hull and this strong superstructure seeks to force the hull downwards into the seabed. The bow, however, resting on the shallower foundations, is stopping that happening. The inexorable downward pull of the mass of the ship is placing huge strain on the hull and it is starting to show the effects at its weakest points, just forward and aft of the armoured superstructure, the 'citadel'. In these two locations, the hull is giving way and is being twisted and buckled. At deck level the hull noticeably sweeps upwards towards the stem into shallower water.

One of the unusual features of the *Hood* is the large section of hull forward of the superstructure that angles back at 45 degrees towards the main deck. When the ship was underway her massive anchors were winched up and secured on these flat-angled sections to avoid any damage to her hull. Her massive anchor hawse pipes just forward are a tangible reminder to divers of the scale and majesty of this pre-dreadnought battleship.

The hull and main deck sweep upwards towards the very stem at the bow itself. Whilst on the bottom there was no kelp to obscure the wreck, as divers move upwards towards the shallower bow, the jumble of foundation blocks becomes carpeted with thick stands of kelp that wave with the gentle current.

Reaching the bow, it becomes clear that only a few metres of the stem, down from the deck, are left in situ and that a large section down to her (now higher) keel is now missing. If a tide is running and forced to squeeze itself through the gaps at either end of the wreck, it is common to find a large shoal of bib holding position in the current here.

DIVE DETAILS FOR THE BRITISH PRE-DREADNOUGHT BATTLESHIP HMS *HOOD*

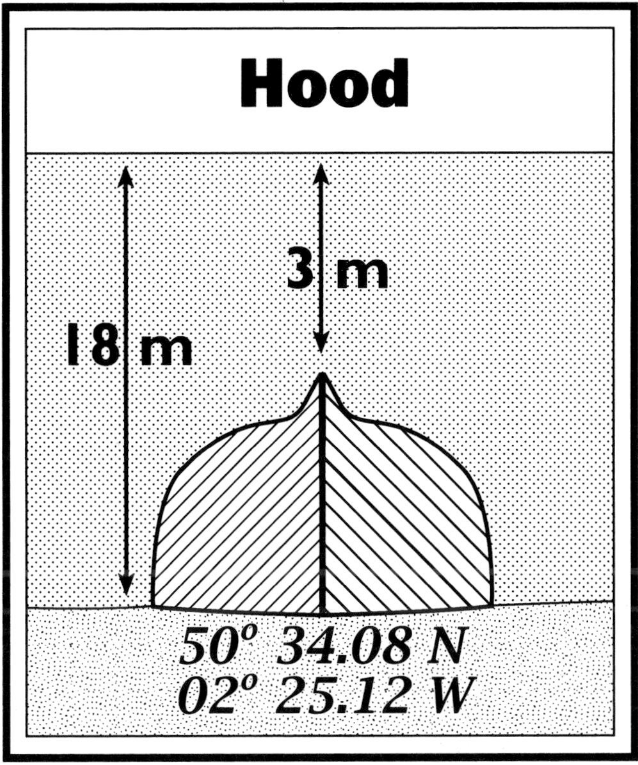

Divers have now travelled the length of the ship on the seabed and it is possible to rise up to the bow section of the hull towards the surface. In this area the damage caused by the inexorable downward pull of her massive weight can be seen. It appears that the entire hull almost to the stern has moved downwards by several metres. The break in the hull just forward of her superstructure does however allow some views inside into the jumbled remains of this pre-dreadnought's innards and machinery.

Moving further aft, the engine-room has noticeably collapsed inwards over recent years but the huge boilers, crankshafts and gear wheels are still open to view and impressive. Further aft still, divers have returned to where the dive started. The free section of the port-side prop shaft has broken from its mounts and lies at an unnatural angle just forward of the imposing rudder.

More stone blocks rest against the hull, filling the gap between the stern and breakwater.

The remains of HMS *Hood* today provide a haven for all types of sealife which find both food and shelter in its cavernous spaces and intricate nooks and crannies. During a typical dive it is common to see pollack, lobsters, cod, bass, pipe-fish, the occasional seal and the largest spider crabs I have ever seen. Whilst like all wrecks *Hood* is best dived at slack water, most diving takes place on the southern or seaward side of the wreck, where divers are protected from any current by the vast bulk of the wreck.

There are not many other locations in the world where you can dive with such ease on such a huge relic of a bygone era, just a few minutes by boat from shore. The remains of HMS *Hood* are a veritable time capsule, a glimpse into an era before the dawn of the dreadnought.

ESSENTIAL INFORMATION

SHORE DIVING: The wreck can be dived from the shore entering the water on the south side of the breakwater. Descend by small buoy and follow guide rope to the stern of the wreck.

BOAT LAUNCH SITE: The wreck can be dived from RIB and hard boat. It is dangerous for vessels to attempt to pass over the wreck itself. Small boats can pass with care between the stern of the wreck close to the southern pier.

HARD BOAT DIVING: Shuttle trips to dive HMS *Hood* are run by a number of operators, including: From Portland – Breakwater Diving Centre (01305) 860269, The Scuba Centre (01305) 826666, Underwater Explorers (01305) 824555, Portland Oceaneering Ltd (01305) 860402, Fathom & Blues (01305) 826789; from Weymouth – *Channel Chieftain* (01305) 787155, *Skin Deep* (01305) 782556, Old Harbour Dive Centre (01305) 760888, *Kyarratoo* (07774) 993326), *Wey Chieftain, Dive Time, Diver City.*

TIDAL CONDITIONS: For training dives this wreck should be dived at slack water. More experienced divers will be able to cope with the current at other times and use the shelter provided by the wreck.

VISIBILITY: In winter and during the May plankton bloom, visibility can close down to 1–2 metres. Average summer visibility is about 5 metres.

MAXIMUM DEPTH: 18msw.

LEAST DEPTH: 2–3msw on upturned whale back of keel.

COASTGUARD: Portland and Weymouth Coastguard (01305) 760439.

RECOMPRESSION FACILITIES: Poole Hyperbaric Hotline (01426) 316636. Institute of Naval Medicine Gosport Hotline (07831) 151523.

AIR SUPPLIES: In Portland, Breakwater Diving Centre (01305) 860269 offer air, nitrox and trimix. Fathom & Blues, The Scuba Centre, Underwater Explorers, Portland Oceaneering Ltd (tel. nos. above).

In Weymouth, Old Harbour Dive Centre (01305) 760888.

HYDROGRAPHIC CHART: Approaches to Portland and Weymouth, No 2255, Berry Head to Bill of Portland, No 3315.

POSITION: Lat 50.34.08 N, Long 002 25.12 W.

DIVER LEVEL: This wreck is suitable for all levels of diver from novice to experienced wreck diver.

Chapter 3

HMS/M *M2*, Lyme Bay, Dorset

The wreck of HMS/M *M2* is unique. She is a 296-feet-long British submarine, one of the four M class submarines laid down in 1916 during the dark days of the First World War. She lies in easily accessible and relatively shallow waters not far offshore and is a glimpse of a hugely innovative and far-sighted development in submarine warfare, at a time when the full potential of the submarine as a weapon of war was being explored.

Traditionally, submarines had used mines, torpedoes or a

HMS/M *M2* launching the world's smallest seaplane, a Parnell Peto. Photo courtesy of the Royal Navy Submarine Museum

small deck-mounted gun on the surface to sink enemy ships. Sometimes the submarine would approach a smaller unarmed enemy merchant vessel on the surface and send a boarding party onto the vessel to sink it by planting explosives or grenades, thus saving a precious torpedo for larger prey.

What made the M class so radically different was that for the first time the British Navy were going to mount a huge 12-inch battleship gun on the submarine's foredeck. Battleships until then had always given away their position by the tell-tale thick black plume of smoke from their coal-fired furnaces. However, the M class submarines with their lethal 12-inch battleship gun would be able to approach their target submerged and unseen, using stealth to get into a firing position that traditional surface vessels would not be allowed to get into. They would then be able to leave the scene of the attack submerged and undetected.

M2 originally began its life as *K19*, ordered by the Royal Navy as part of the 1916 War Emergency Programme. She displaced 1,594 tons surfaced, 1,946 tons submerged. She was a large submarine, some 90.1 metres in length, with a beam of 7.5 metres and a draft of 4.9 metres. She was fitted out with two Vickers 12-cylinder diesel engines developing 2,400hp. She also had two electric motors for submerged running – these developed 1,600hp. On the surface, her twin shafts could push her to speeds of 15 knots. Submerged she could achieve 9 knots. Her maximum diving depth was 75 metres. *M2* had an effective range of 3,840 nautical miles and an endurance of 20 days. She carried 6 officers and 59 ratings. She also carried eight deadly 18-inch torpedoes for her four bow tubes. The 12-inch battleship gun was originally intended for coastal bombardment.

Although *M2* was laid down in 1916, her construction was not completed until after the war, in 1920. Her 12-inch gun was subsequently removed in 1927 and in its place, in another radical piece of lateral thinking, a watertight hangar for a small seaplane was added forward of the conning tower.

The idea was so novel that it was recognised for its brilliance worldwide and instantly gave submarines an entirely new role to play in naval warfare. HMS/M *M2* was lost during routine sea exercises off Portland in 1932, however. She sank into 35 metres of water, coming to rest on an even keel. She remains almost completely intact and is a rare opportunity to dive an entirely different sort of submarine, from the days when anything was possible – in theory.

To understand HMS/M *M2* it is necessary to know something of her sister submarine, the first of the M class, *M1*. She was laid down in 1916 at the Vickers Yard at Barrow originally as the *K18*. She was, however, altered to house a 12-

inch gun from a scuttled King Edward VII class battleship, HMS *Formidable* – it was a breathtaking idea, as the biggest gun on a submarine until that time had been a 5-inch. But this was the era of the dreadnought, of battleships and battle cruisers – the Big Gun ruled the seas. A submarine that could approach an enemy unseen and fire from a submerged position with only the top of the barrel and its bead sight projecting above the water was certainly revolutionary and a potentially devastating idea. There were drawbacks however – only one shot could be fired as the sub had to surface to reload.

The First World War drew to a close before HMS/M *M1* was completed and ready for action. Nevertheless, *M1* was developed in the post-war years with many firings of her 60-ton 12-inch gun, not all without incident. On a few occasions water got into her barrel and blew off several feet at the muzzle end.

In November 1925 a submarine exercise was held in the Channel off Devon. HMS/M *M1* took part along with the submarines *H22*, *H29*, *H30*, *H34*, the submarine depot ship *Maidstone* and submarine tender *Alecto*. On Friday, 13 November, *M1* did not respond to radio calls, nor did she report in when she should have. A huge search swung into operation but no trace of her was found. Divers were sent down on every seabed obstruction in the area she was last known to be, but their efforts proved useless as they just found one old wreck after another. There was no trace whatsoever of *M1*.

Shortly after, however, the 2,159-ton Swedish steamship *Vidar* completed a passage to Stockholm which had taken her through the area in which *M1* had been exercising. Captain Anell felt his vessel had suffered damage after striking a submerged object at about 8 p.m. on 12 November, the evening before the alert. The *Vidar* was put into dry dock. When her plates were exposed, bent and damaged plating at her bow was revealed along with tell-tale traces of grey paint that matched that of *M1*. The search was called off and the memory of *M1* passed into the history books.

In recent years her wreck was found and dived by technical divers who have concluded that *M1* did indeed collide with the *Vidar*, which struck the submarine's 12-inch gun. A port from the gun passed directly through the pressure hull. As a result, when the gun was dislodged during the impact this opening was exposed to the sea. The hull flooded and she was sent to the bottom.

The second of the M class, HMS/M *M2*, was completed after the war in 1920, also with the intention of carrying a big 12-inch battleship gun. In 1927, two years after the loss of *M1*, the 12-inch gun was removed and in the space where the gun and its mounting had been situated, just forward of the conning tower, a watertight aeroplane hangar was fitted to house the Parnell Peto, one of the smallest seaplanes in the world at the time, with wings which folded to allow her to be secured and stowed away in the hangar. This purpose-designed two-seat seaplane was manufactured by George Parnell and Co. and fitted initially with a three-cylinder and latterly a five-cylinder 135hp engine. Two Petos were initially built, *N181* and *N182*, although others such as *N255* were subsequently used on the vessel. The seaplane was launched by catapult off a runway on *M2*'s foredeck.

The seaplane's role was to serve as a stealth reconnaissance aircraft that could appear without warning at locations outwith normal air-cover range, spot a foe or target and then, as if by magic, disappear beneath the waves again. On its return to *M2*, the Peto landed in the sea near the submarine and was then hoisted aboard by a small crane before being stowed in its hangar.

HMS/M *M2* served for five years in this role of submarine aircraft carrier before her ultimate doom in January 1932. Her crew became very experienced at rising up from depth and checking via the periscope that it was safe to surface, before breaking the surface, opening the hangar doors and catapulting the seaplane aloft. There was,

THE PARNELL PETO, WINGS NOW EXTENDED, IS READIED FOR FLIGHT.
PHOTO COURTESY OF THE ROYAL NAVY SUBMARINE MUSEUM

however, one incident in 1930 when her seaplane crashed on the beach at Gosport shortly after taking off, to the alarm of holidaymakers.

On 26 January 1932, *M2* left Portland harbour on exercise just after 9 a.m. in calm conditions but with a little fog about. Her role that day was initially to exercise alone in West Bay before rendezvousing with the submarines *L67* and *L71* from Portsmouth for combined exercises.

Just after 10 a.m., Lieutenant-Commander J.D. Leathes, in command of *M2*, sent a signal to the vessel co-ordinating the exercise, HMS *Titania*: 'I am going to dive.'

The hours then passed by and it was some time before the busy wireless operators on HMS *Titania*, swamped by messages from the exercise, realised that no further communication had been received from *M2*. Even then it was felt that this was probably due to a communications problem. However, when *M2* failed to return to Portland harbour at her scheduled time of 4.15 p.m. it was clear that there was a real problem.

At 5.30 p.m. the destroyers HMS *Torrid, Thruster, Rowena* and *Salmon* left port to start a search of the area in which *M2* had been exercising. It was possible that she was simply disabled and unable to communicate, but still on the surface. At 7 p.m. the submarines *H44* and *H49* joined the search. Just before 8 p.m., with *M2* not having been located on the surface, a full-scale emergency was declared and seamen in the area were recalled to their ships to start a search. Theatre and cinema shows ashore were halted and managers went onstage to make the recall announcements. Cars and coaches were sent from Portland to Weymouth to ferry crewmen back to their ships.

By 9 p.m. some 500 men had returned to their ships. They knew that if *M2* had sunk she could be sitting on the seabed with her crew still alive. Her air supplies would soon start to dwindle but there was sufficient for her crew to survive for another 48 hours submerged. It was a deadly race against time to locate the submarine and rescue her crew. There was also an added reason for extreme urgency. *M2* was carrying the latest free-ascent lifesaving equipment, the new Davis Escape Apparatus, which would allow her crew to exit the sunken submarine and rise up to the surface. This newly developed safety equipment had been used in earnest for the first time only the year before, when HMS *Poseidon* was sunk following a collision off the coast of China. Many of her crew were able to escape safely from her sunken hull. It was possible that at any time the crew of *M2* might also escape from the sunken hull using this equipment and rise up to the surface. With cold water and treacherous currents they wouldn't last long exposed to the elements. The sub had to be found and vessels be present to pick up any escapees.

Just after midnight the Admiralty announced that a contact had been located:

> An object, presumed to be the submarine *M2*, has been located three miles west of Portland Bill, in 17 fathoms, on a sandy bottom. Salvage craft and divers have been sent from Portsmouth to this position with the utmost despatch.

The destroyer HMS *Sabre* carrying Navy hardhat divers specially trained for working with submarines left Portsmouth and hurried to the scene at 25 knots. She expected to be on site by 2 a.m. that morning.

Two submarine salvage ships also set out for the site and were expected to arrive on station at around dawn. It was felt that unless there had been a catastrophic breach of the hull the crew were probably at this stage still alive and well inside the sunken submarine. If so, then they would be working to right any mechanical problem to allow *M2* to rise up to the surface again under her own power. They would not abandon the vessel until every hope of refloating the submarine was gone. At that stage they would then have to use the Davis Escape Apparatus.

By the afternoon of the following day, 27 January, however, the mood of the rescuers was turning very gloomy. Telegrams had been sent to the families of all members of the crew, their stark, bare lines striking fear into those who received them:

> Regret to inform you that your husband is missing and feared drowned in submarine *M2*, believed sunk off Portland on Tuesday.

The Navy hardhat divers from HMS *Sabre* started their descent down to the contact that was believed to be the stricken sub, but heavy tides and seas made it impossible for them to reach the contact – they got down to a depth of 70 feet, some 30 feet short of the bottom.

That night, at 10.30 p.m, the Admiralty issued a statement confirming that the divers' attempts to reach the contact had failed due to the conditions but that diving would continue throughout the night where possible. Meantime the Admiralty had received some intriguing reports that the captain of a coaster that had just arrived at Gravelines, near Calais, had seen what was believed to be *M2* shortly before she disappeared. Importantly, he had asked in conversation whether it was usual for a submarine to dive stern-first, as that was what he had seen in West Bay, off Chesil Beach, Portland Bill.

Early the next day, 28 January, a *Daily Mail* reporter traced the captain – before the Admiralty had done so. He was able to give new information to the Admiralty that challenged the assumptions on the basis of which the search had been carried out so far. He sent a despatch from Gravelines:

> I have just had the first interview with Captain A.E. Howard of the Newcastle-on-Tyne steamer, *Tynesider*, the last vessel to see the *M2* before she disappeared. I found him asleep in his cabin just after midnight two miles off Gravelines harbour, which the *Tynesider* will only be able to enter at 3 a.m. 'There can be no doubt,' Mr Howard said to me, 'that the submarine I saw yesterday morning is the same which disappeared off Portland. I was coming from Charleston, Cornwall, with a cargo of China clay yesterday at 11.30 a.m. As I was getting near Portland I saw the submarine. I could read quite clearly her mark, 'M'. She was on top of the water. Before I could approach I saw her sink rather suddenly, her stern first. I did not pay too much attention to it at first, since I had never seen a submarine dive. However, when I called at Portland at 2.30 p.m. I told the news to a man on the quayside and asked him if it was the right way for a submarine to go down. He said he had never seen a ship sink, so I did not trouble any more. When I left the harbour I met a submarine going in and I thought that it was the one I had seen earlier and that everything was all right. Of course I was sorry to learn this evening on the wireless that *M2* was lost. But the position the Admiralty gave is not a good one. When I saw the *M2* she was approximately eight miles NW by N from Portland Bill, two and a half miles from shore. I am afraid they are searching in the wrong place.

By 8 a.m. that morning the Admiralty announced that although they had made no progress diving the original contact that night, they were now giving attention to the position that had been reported by the captain of the *Tynesider* and also given by another vessel, the *Crown of Denmark*. The captain of the *Crown of Denmark* had reported seeing a brilliant white flash, repeated two or three times, followed by a loud report that echoed over the water. He reported the position as soon as he put into Portland and the position turned out to be within half a mile of the position reported by the *Tynesider* – not far at all in the days of dead reckoning and approximate positions.

The Navy continued trying to identify and dive targets in West Bay, which was also ominously known as the Bay of a Thousand Wrecks. It was a colossal task, using the location methods of the time, a wire sweep to snag underwater obstructions and then sending divers down to identify.

At 8.30 p.m. that day the Admiralty announced that it was abandoning attempts to dive the first contact as the sweep kept slipping and divers could not reach it. Diving went on all through the night in a desperate race against time – all knew that even if the hull were intact the air supplies would soon run out.

At 5 a.m. the next day, 29 January, the Admiralty announced that the first obstruction discovered had now been dived and found to be an old wreck. They would however continue sweeping in that vicinity as an earlier sweep had brought up a pair of submarine hand flags in a canvas case, although they bore no distinguishing marks. Ominously, the announcement concluded, 'No hope now of saving life.'

That evening the Admiralty made a further announcement that all the obstructions examined by divers that day had turned out to be old wrecks. The search however would continue for the time being. Then, later, the Admiralty announced that it was no longer possible to hope for the rescue of any of the officers and men on board. A list was issued of the 7 officers and 53 petty officers and ratings whose 'death must therefore now be presumed'.

For the following five days the continuous regime of laboriously searching for a contact and then sending divers down to check failed to reveal the resting place of *M2*. Each time divers went down they reported an old wreck – there were believed to be at least 200 in West Bay itself. But the search continued relentlessly in an effort to find the sub and learn what had caused its loss.

Then, on 1 February 1932, Commander H.M. Daniel commented to the press that it was possible that *M2* had been practising getting her small plane launched in the minimum of time after an unseen submerged approach to a supposed enemy. He went on that it was possible that over-keen crew may have attempted to gain access to the hangar from within, a second or two before the submarine was fully up. It was well known that the crew of the *M2* were very proud of the speed with which they could do this and were constantly trying to beat their own record. The front doors of the hangar, although watertight, were a large flat surface. If they had in any way leaked whilst the vessel was submerged it was possible that 200–300 tons of water may have accumulated in the hangar unknown to the crew. On opening the hatch from the pressure hull into the hangar, that water may have poured down in an overwhelming deluge into the submarine, causing it to sink by the stern. If this theory was right then everyone in the submarine would have drowned almost at once.

On 2 February newspapers ran a story of a fisherman who had reported picking up the body of a man in a white submarine-issue sweater in West Bay. The body had fallen back into the sea whilst attempts were being made to retrieve it and had been lost. The same day the Admiralty reported that the Navy had retrieved a cap belonging to the coxswain of the *M2* floating in a canvas bag and then on a sweep wire a collar belonging to a chief petty officer. The search was closing in.

On 3 February, the Admiralty announced that *M2* had been found: 'The Rear-Admiral Submarines has reported that he has located Submarine *M2* in position 50 degrees 31.2 min N., 5.8 miles from Portland Bill.'

Divers had been sent down from the destroyer HMS *Torrid* which had located a contact with sub-like characteristics on its Asdic listening equipment. At first the divers couldn't reach the contact because of strong currents and poor visibility, but after further attempts they reached the obstruction and confirmed that it was indeed the *M2*, sitting in 18 fathoms of water with her stern in the sand and shingle and her bow raised off the seabed to such an extent that divers could walk underneath. The divers also reported that the hangar door and the upper conning tower hatch were open and that the forward hatch and engine-room hatch were closed.

Immediately, salvage plans to lift the submarine started to be prepared. It did however seem likely from these reports that perhaps the hangar doors had been opened too early – before the submarine was fully on the surface. If the inside hangar hatch was also open then water would rush into the hull of the sub causing it to go down stern-first.

At this point Ernest Cox, the legendary salver of the scuttled German First World War High Seas Fleet at Scapa Flow, offered his services to the Admiralty. His offer was accepted immediately. After all, he held the record for the greatest feat of maritime salvage ever, having raised the majority of the 74 scuttled German warships of the High Seas Fleet: 26,000-ton battlecruisers, battleships, cruisers, light cruisers and torpedo boats had all been raised up from depths ranging up to 45 metres. These ships had been sitting on the seabed in a bewildering variety of ways. Some lay on their keels, some on their sides and some upside down. If he could do that then surely he could lift a small submarine in shallower water with an intact pressure hull.

The sunken monsters of Scapa Flow were nearly all lifted by divers manually sealing all the openings in their hulls, guns and superstructures with concrete. Divers then entered the hull and sealed off an internal compartment, which was then filled with compressed air. Air locks, sometimes 100 feet long, were made up of old boilers welded together to form a vertical tunnel. These were then welded to the hull above the airtight inner compartment to allow salvage workers to descend down ladders inside the boiler air lock tunnel and enter the air-filled section of the hull of the sunken giant. Working inside the hull, sometimes 150 feet below the surface, these salvers, in very harsh and dangerous conditions, would then strip the area and make it ready for a lift to the surface. Divers would seal off the next area of hull and blow compressed air into it, and the salvers would then move into this area to repeat the process.

Once the laborious process of fully clearing and sealing the hull internally was completed, the workmen were recalled to the surface and compressed air was blown into the hull. Any remaining water was forced out and the hull became buoyant. Breaking free from the suction of the seabed the hulls would rush up to the surface amidst a foam of escaping, expanding air.

Cox felt that *M2* should not present too much difficulty. He arrived at Portland and met the divers and salvage crew on 7 February. He briefed them as to how he planned to use the same method that he had used at Scapa – seal all the hull openings and pump the hull full of compressed air. Confidently he told them that *M2* would be on the surface within a week.

The following day, 8 February, divers from HMS *Tedworth* descended to *M2*. It was considered too dangerous for the divers to enter the hangar – which still had the seaplane in situ – as there was too great a risk of entanglement of their air hoses. To minimise the risk, steel hawsers from the powerful tug *Kennet* were fixed to the seaplane. The *Kennet* then moved ahead and the seaplane was torn from the hangar and dragged to the surface.

The weather was starting to break and although divers were able to start sealing the conning tower hatch, Cox had to revise his estimate of when he would have *M2* on the surface. The work continued until the weather got so bad that mooring buoys were broken free. Eventually the work had to be suspended.

On 4 March HMS *Tedworth* returned to the site but foul weather again forced work to halt temporarily. Soon, however, it was reported that the salvage preparations were almost complete and it would be possible to lift the submarine shortly. As the work progressed, some of the unfortunate crew were found. On 14 March a body was found in the hangar, then another on 18 March. More open hatches were found which required to be closed then sealed by having concrete poured over them. The work was difficult in the dark and strongly tidal conditions with constant setbacks.

On 3 April *M2* was still sitting on the bottom and Cox reported that the hatch inside the hangar was indeed open, as was the conning tower hatch. These had now been sealed. It was then reported that the engine-room hatch behind the conning tower was open – and then that the hatch in the crew's quarters was also open. Each hatch was closed down with a steel jack. Then, concrete was poured over it to stop it opening during the lift as compressed air was pumped into the hull. Divers were also busy cutting holes in the pressure hull under the engine-room and other areas to allow water to escape as air filled the hull during the lift.

In June a new difficulty was found – some of the ballast tanks could not be pumped clear of water. Only 7 of the 18 were suitable for compressed air to be

COX'S WORKERS PREPARE A LARGE PONTOON ON THE SHORE FOR USE IN RECOVERING *M2*.
PHOTO COURTESY OF THE IMPERIAL WAR MUSEUM, LONDON

THE PONTOON IS MANOEUVRED INTO POSITION ABOVE *M2*.
PHOTO COURTESY OF THE IMPERIAL WAR MUSEUM, LONDON

THE PONTOON IS DEPLOYED DURING ATTEMPT TO LIFT *M2* FROM THE SEABEAD.
PHOTO COURTESY OF THE IMPERIAL WAR MUSEUM, LONDON

blown into them. On 1 July the body of Leading Aircraftman Leslie Gregory in full flying kit was found about 15 feet away from the sub – it was assumed that he had been getting ready to man the seaplane when the sub had sunk and that his body had been pulled out of the hangar when the seaplane itself was dragged out.

By November repeated attempts to raise the sub had been foiled by bad weather and operating difficulties. By the beginning of December however preparations were finalised for a last attempt to lift *M2*. The compressors were started at 11 a.m. on 7 December, and compressed air was pumped into the hull. It would be a lengthy procedure to fill her sufficiently so that she would become buoyant and lift to the surface – and it had been set up so that she would rise on an even keel with her upper works breaking the surface first.

Finally she did lift off the bottom, at first on an even keel. Shortly into the ascent however things started to go wrong and her stern lifted higher. At 3.20 p.m. those on the surface saw two pontoons and the stern of the submarine break the surface amid a boiling lather of bubbles from the compressed air.

M2 reached an equilibrium sitting with her bow resting on the seabed, and her buoyant stern settling just under the surface. Frantic efforts to pump more air into the bow section to lift it up failed. As darkness spread over the scene the salvers gave up and lowered the stern to the seabed. The following day, 8 December 1932, the Admiralty announced that it had abandoned the salvage operations. *M2* and her crew would be allowed to rest on the seabed.

The subsequent Admiralty investigation concluded that *M2* had foundered as she surfaced and prepared to launch her seaplane. The main hangar door had been opened perhaps too early. The position of the seaplane still in its hangar – and of the crew found aboard – suggested that they were getting the plane ready for flight as *M2* surfaced. The main pressure hull was undamaged, so water must have entered through the open main hangar door and then through the hatch from the hull below into the hangar – which was also found to be open. It was known that the hangar door and hatch were at times open simultaneously to allow communication between the hangar and the rating operating the hangar door. There was no voice pipe to allow such communications, a possible design fault. *M2* was after all an experimental development craft.

Another crucial design failing was that the hatch between the hangar and the pressure hull could only be closed from within the hangar itself and not from within the pressure hull. As a result, if the hangar became flooded with the hatch open, it could not be closed. It seems likely that a combination of design faults

THE HAUNTING REMAINS OF THE WRECK OF
THE *SALSETTE* LIE AT THE BOTTOM OF LYME BAY
© ROD MACDONALD 2003

THE COLOSSAL REMAINS OF THE BRITISH PRE-DREADNOUGHT BATTLESHIP HMS *HOOD* STILL BLOCK THE SOUTHERN ENTRANCE TO PORTLAND HARBOUR

THE ATMOSPHERIC AND MOODY WRECK OF HMS/M *M2*, IN LYME BAY

THE WRECK OF THE ONCE-BEAUTIFUL SS *KYARRA*, ISLE OF PURBECK, DOREST

THE WRECK OF THE SS *MAINE*, OFF BOLT HEAD, SOUTH DEVON

THE WRECK OF THE BEAUTIFUL SCHOONER-RIGGED SS *BRETAGNE*,
IN BABBACOMBE BAY, EAST DEVON

THE HAUNTING REMAINS OF THE BRITISH LINER
MOLDAVIA, OFF LITTLEHAMPTON, WEST SUSSEX

THE MASSIVE REMAINS OF THE *ALAUNIA* LIE IN 35MSW,
A FEW MILES OFFSHORE FROM HASTINGS, EAST SUSSEX

THE REMAINS OF THE SS *MONGOLIAN* LIE IN THE
DARK DEPTHS OF FILEY BAY, YORKSHIRE

THE REMAINS OF THE AMERICAN LIBERTY SHIP
JAMES EAGAN LAYNE IN WHITSAND BAY, CORNWALL

THE ATMOSPHERIC AND MOODY WRECK OF HMS/M *M2*. © ROD MACDONALD 2003

and over-eager enthusiasm to get the seaplane launched resulted in the hangar door being opened when the sea level around was still too high. The hangar flooded and water poured down into the pressure hull, fatally altering *M2*'s buoyancy. This caused her stern to sink as the water rushed aftwards. Her bows reared up and led to what the captain of the *Tynesider* saw as the stern-first dive.

Today the wreck of the submarine *M2* lies in 30–35msw some 4.74 nautical miles from Portland harbour on a bearing of 281 degrees. This is not however the original position she was lost in, as she was moved during the salvage works detailed above. It takes the hard boats operating from Portland harbour about 30–40 minutes to reach the site, RIBs being able to do it in half that time.

M2 sits on an even keel on a sandy seabed with her bows pointing to the north-west and her stern to the south-east. She is a spectacular dive on a unique developmental submarine that is now nearly 90 years old. To the best of my knowledge you can't dive a First World War vintage submarine fitted out with an aeroplane hangar anywhere else in the world.

M2 is a very atmospheric dive for a number of reasons. Once I reached the wreck I was immediately struck by how large the wreck actually is. On my first dive on her, despite having read dive reports previously, it was clear that I had not really appreciated her true scale in advance. In my own mind I had expected a far smaller vessel. The sheer size of her, 90 metres in length and 7.5 metres in the beam, makes her width and length not far short of a small steamship such as the SS *Hispania* in the Sound of Mull. She is a *big* submarine.

Additionally, although the average underwater visibility over the summer months would be 5-plus metres, she does lie in a silty area in which almost all of the ambient light reaching down from the surface is filtered out by the particles in suspension. This makes her an often dark,

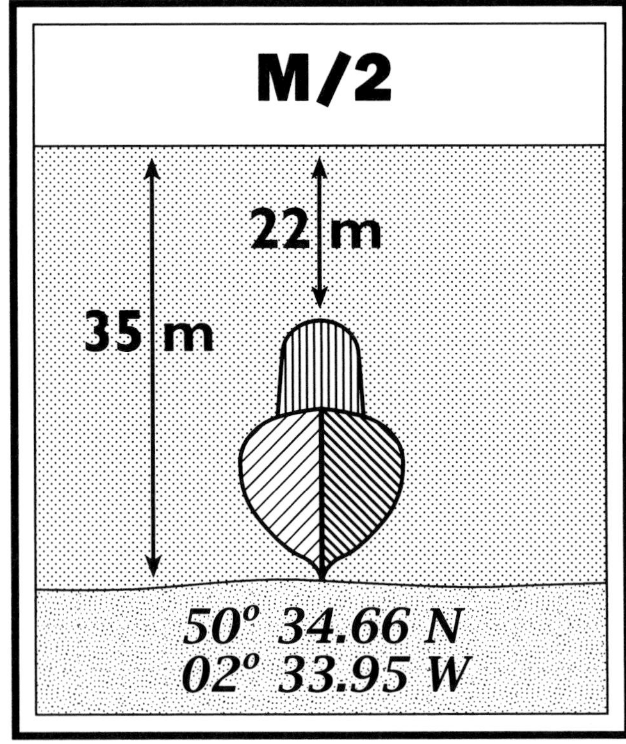

DIVE DETAILS FOR THE WRECK OF HMS/M *M2*

gloomy dive, the sort most British wreck-divers are familiar with. At first as you descend down the shotline the water appears to have a greenish/grey feel to it. Very quickly your surroundings darken as you descend – beneath you it is pitch black, with the shotline seemingly disappearing straight down beneath you into an inky void.

The darkening water slowly turns to jet black around you, the only light being the strong beam of your torch which sweeps around like a light sabre, tirelessly seeking out the first glimpse of metal beneath. Slowly the darkness below seems to acquire a form and gradually the huge hull of *M2* materialises out of the gloom. Other than the small sections of the wreck illuminated by your dive torch beam, divers are cocooned in a black void, their eyes not yet adjusted to their new surroundings. As the minutes of the dive itself pass by, so the divers' night vision kicks in. Eyes become more sensitive and can soon pick out the silhouette of the submarine against the surroundings and distant surface.

The gloominess of the dive itself seems to lends poignancy to the tragic story of those poor seamen who became trapped inside the submarine as she made her terrifying plunge to the seabed. The crew were trapped inside the hull as tons of cold water poured in relentlessly and the submarine quickly impacted onto the seabed and settled. The lights would have soon faded and the hull pitched into total darkness. The inrushing water would have quickly displaced all the air inside the hull. The terror of the end met by the crew is never far away from the minds of divers as they drift over her silent, still remains.

M2 sits on an even keel and the bulky, 7.5-metre-wide pressure hull remains completely intact. The hull narrows and sweeps up to the very sharp, sheer bow itself, sitting well off the seabed. On either side of her sheer stem are set rectangular openings in the hull. These lead back into the hull to a flat bulkhead which has two of her four 18-inch torpedo tubes set in it on either side, one above the other.

Back from the torpedo tubes on her starboard side can be found a small anchor still snugly stowed away in its hawse pipe. Aft of that the bow-diving plane still sits in position. Moving aft from here, divers can move onto the top of the pressure hull where the remains of the seaplane launching ramp runs fore and aft along the top of the hull. The seaplane's floats fitted on either side of this ramp. The Carey compressed air catapult still sits in place at the front of the tracks. It is remarkable how short in fact these tracks are, considering that in this short distance the catapult would get a seaplane airborne from a standing start.

The tracks lead back to the large hangar that is an integral part of the conning tower behind. The hangar door is long gone and the door opening itself stands some 8 feet high. The silt-filled innards of the hangar can be lit up by powerful dive torches.

Above the large hangar doorway a section of the steel girder used for craning the seaplane back onto the submarine still juts proudly forwards along the centre line of the vessel, set on its rotating mount and wracking system. Aft of the hangar itself stands the conning tower, the highest part of the wreck with a depth of 22–24msw. Drifting over this area divers can see the swept combing and the open area immediately behind where officers would stand when she was on the surface. The two periscopes still stand upright, silhouetted against the faint light from the distant surface.

The conning tower sweeps round to a very sharp V-shaped end, marking the start of the expansive stern section of the hull. The rotted remains of handrail uprights still stick up in places, now razor sharp and ready to snag the unwary.

The lengthy aft section of the hull here sweeps back towards the stern where the stern diving planes are still in place. The very stern itself is peculiar to *M2*, very characteristic, narrow and somewhat like the stern of a schooner. Beneath the overhanging stern, the rudder disappears into the seabed. Her twin prop shafts are still visible, on either side of the rudder, their mounting brackets still visible.

The size of the *M2* means that it is possible to completely circumnavigate the wreck in one dive at seabed level or on the pressure hull before heading back to the hangar and conning tower to spend the remaining bottom time exploring these higher areas.

Like most of the Channel wrecks, *M2* should be dived at slack water. If it is slack down on the wreck at the beginning of the dive, by the time a diver's bottom time is finished and the ascent commenced, the tide will have turned and divers will feel the current picking up. Most divers diving this wreck will be carrying out varying amounts of decompression stops on the ascent and so if all divers try to ascend the shotline and carry out their decompression stops on it, the shotline will become congested and uncomfortable. Most dive boat skippers will be happy for you to ascend on delayed deco buoys, drifting freely with the prevailing current.

Essential Information

BOAT LAUNCH SITE: For RIBs slips are available at Weymouth, Portland, West Bay and Lyme Regis. Harbour and launch fees payable.

HARD BOAT DIVING: In Portland – Breakwater Diving Centre (01305) 860269, The Scuba Centre (01305) 826666, Underwater Explorers (01305) 824555, Portland Oceaneering Ltd (01305) 860402, Fathom & Blues (01305) 826789.

LOCAL PORTLAND HARD BOAT *TOPGUN* TAKES A PARTY OF DIVERS OUT TO *M2*. PHOTO: AUTHOR'S COLLECTION

In Weymouth – Old Harbour Dive Centre (01305) 760888, *Channel Chieftain* (01305) 787155, *Skin Deep* (01305) 782556, *Kyarratoo* (07774) 993326.

TIDAL CONDITIONS: Dive at slack water.

VISIBILITY: Average 5–10 metres.

MAXIMUM DEPTH: 35msw.

LEAST DEPTH: 24msw to top of conning tower.

COASTGUARD: Portland and Weymouth Coastguard (01305) 760439.

RECOMPRESSION FACILITIES: Poole Hyperbaric Hotline (01426) 316636, (03367) 771883. Institute of Naval Medicine Gosport Hotline (07831) 151523.

AIR SUPPLIES: In Portland – Breakwater Diving Centre (01305) 860269, Fathom and Blues (01305) 826789. In Weymouth, Old Harbour Dive Centre (01305) 760888.

HYDROGRAPHIC CHART: Approaches to Portland and Weymouth No 2255, Berry Head to Bill of Portland No 3315.

POSITION: Lat 50 34.660 N, Long 002 33.954 W.

DIVER LEVEL: Given the depth and distance offshore this wreck is for the intermediate to advanced diver.

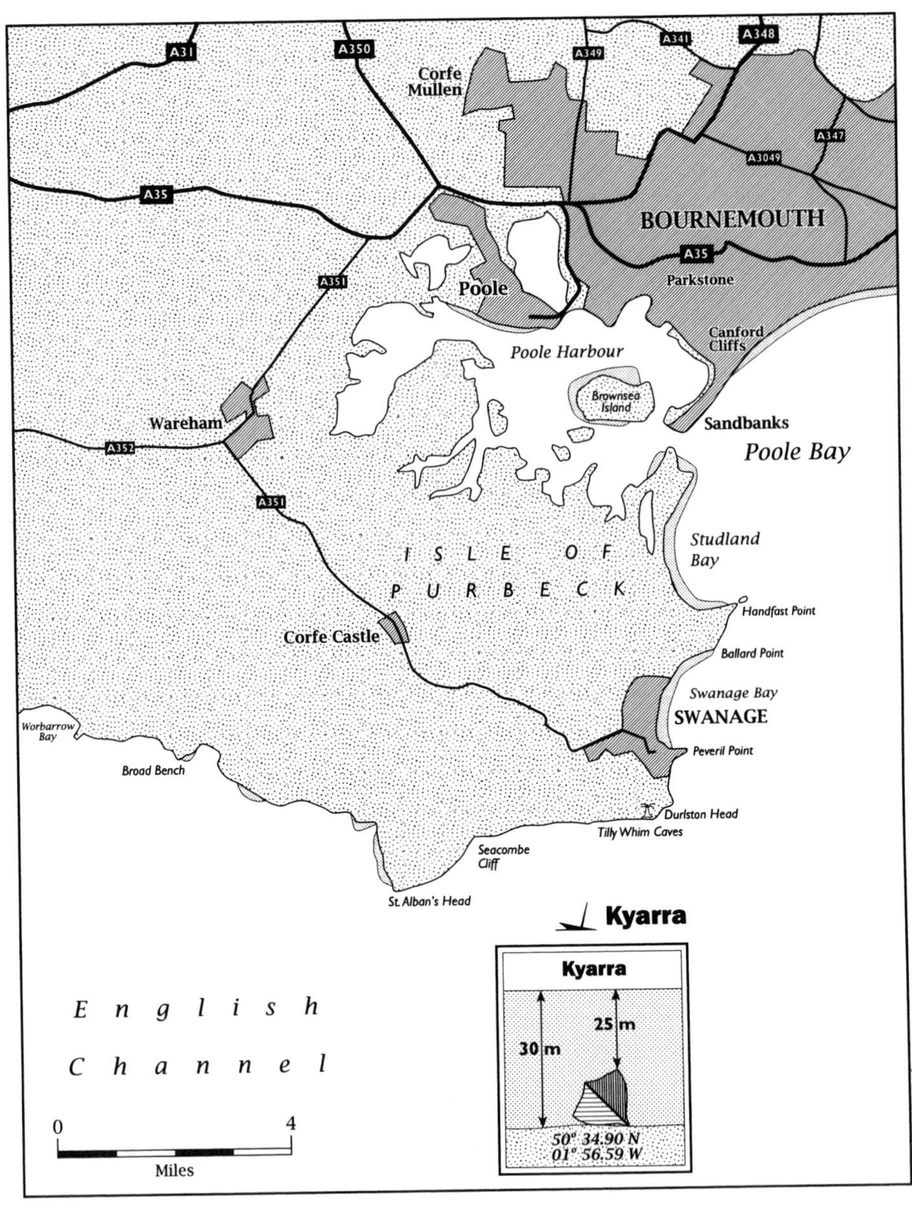
A31
A350
A349
A341
A348
Corfe Mullen
A347
A3049
A35
BOURNEMOUTH
A35
A351
Poole
Parkstone
Canford Cliffs
Poole Harbour
Brownsea Island
Wareham
Sandbanks
Poole Bay
A352
A351
Studland Bay
I S L E O F
P U R B E C K
Handfast Point
Corfe Castle
Ballard Point
Swanage Bay
SWANAGE
Worbarrow Bay
Peveril Point
Broad Bench
Durlston Head
Tilly Whim Caves
Seacombe Cliff
St. Alban's Head
Kyarra
Kyarra
25 m
30 m
50° 34.90 N
01° 56.59 W
English
Channel
0
4
Miles

OPPOSITE: LOCATION CHART FOR SS *KYARRA*, DORSET.

Chapter 4

SS *Kyarra*, Isle of Purbeck, Dorset

THE 6,953-TON SS *KYARRA* IN HER FITTING-OUT DOCK ON THE CLYDE.
PHOTO COURTESY OF THE NATIONAL MARITIME MUSEUM, GREENWICH

Just three days after Oberleutnant Johannes Lohs in *UB-57* had sent the beautiful troopship HMS *Moldavia* (see Chapter Eight) to the bottom of the English Channel in a determined attack, Lohs found himself with another prize in his sights as he looked through *UB-57*'s periscope just to the south of Durlston Head in Swanage Bay, Dorset.

For there, silhouetted in the bright early light of 26 May 1918, was the imposing and majestic outline of the 6,953-ton passenger and cargo-carrying liner SS *Kyarra*.

En route to Australia, she was under orders to proceed to Devonport, Plymouth, where she would embark 1,000 wounded Australian troops – troops who would never be able to fight again and were being returned to Australia. The date of 26 May 1918, however, was a day of destiny for the *Kyarra*. It would be her last day afloat.

—

The steel cargo and passenger luxury liner *Kyarra* was a beautiful twin-masted schooner-rigged steamer built on the River Clyde, Scotland, in 1903 during the classic age of steamship construction by W. Denny Brothers, shipbuilders in Dumbarton. It was the era of opulence, a time when ships were fitted out to the highest and most luxurious of standards. Brass fitments and finishings were everywhere – a style of fitting-out that would diminish in the years immediately preceding the First World War when non-ferrous metals were needed for the arms race.

The *Kyarra* was in fact the second of two vessels built to the same design. Her sister ship the *Kanowna* was completed and launched just four months ahead of the *Kyarra*. The Denny Brother's yard would have resounded for a long time

THE UNIQUE 6-BLADED SCREWS DESIGNED FOR THE *KYARRA*. PHOTO: COURTESY OF THE NATIONAL MARITIME MUSEUM, GREENWICH

to the noises of men working the metal to construct these two fabulous ships, drilling plates, hammering in and tapping rivets. Huge tripod-lifting cranes towered above the ships as they slowly took form, dominating the skyline and the low buildings and shipworkers' houses surrounding the yard itself. These huge vessels and tripods towered over the shipyard workers as they arrived at the yard and departed at the end of their long, noisy and backbreaking day's toil. To the workers, however, it was simply a familiar, daily sight.

The *Kyarra* herself was launched on 2 February 1903 and was then moved into a fitting-out dock where all her finishing touches were added. Once complete, she was delivered to her new owners on 16 April 1903, two weeks ahead of schedule. Costing £144,652, she netted her builders a profit of £6,889. She was an impressive 415 feet 5 inches in length, with a beam of 52 feet 2 inches and a draught of 31 feet 4.5 inches, 6,953 tons gross, with a net tonnage of 4,383. She was fitted with two immense triple-expansion Denny engines which developed 375hp each. The combined 750hp drove her two unique, specially designed, 6-bladed screws to push her through the water at speeds of up to 15.4 knots.

The *Kanowna* and *Kyarra* had been ordered by the Australasian United Steam Navigation Company Limited, who maintained offices in London. The *Kyarra*'s International Code Signal Letters were T.W.S.C. and she was registered at the port of Fremantle, Western Australia, in 1903.

Built to combine carrying cargo and fare-paying passengers, the *Kyarra* was fitted out with 42 first-class 3-berth cabins and 20 second-class cabins of 8 berths each, and a number of well-appointed state rooms. In all, she could carry more than 250 passengers.

The *Kyarra* was constructed with one large superstructure set midships along her hull. At the front of it, rising up for four deck levels, was the main bridge itself which would have held in its lower decks first-class accommodation and lounges, and behind the bridge itself, the captain's accommodation.

Aft of the bridge, cabins ringed around the deckhouse on two levels, surrounding the engine casing and smoke stack which rose up from the engine-room far below decks in the bowels of the ship. On top of this deckhouse wooden lifeboats hung in their davits, fore and aft of the pitched engine-room roof with its skylights.

For her cargo-carrying role, her cavernous holds had a depth of 28 feet 6 inches and were able to hold 253,000 cubic feet of cargo. Sturdy cargo winches were set fore and aft of her foredeck and aft deck holds.

After her launch in 1903 the *Kyarra* entered what was to become a very

THE OPULENT BOAT DECK OF THE SS *KYARRA*. PHOTOS COURTESY OF THE NATIONAL MARITIME MUSEUM, GREENWICH

profitable service for her owners, being based initially in Melbourne. Her first voyage was in August 1903 – from Melbourne to Adelaide, Albany and Fremantle, Perth. She would go on to spend the majority of her pre-war years carrying cargo and passengers around Australian shores, becoming popular with Queensland and western Australian passengers.

After ten years of profitable service, the Great War unleashed itself across Europe. Britain turned to its Empire to supply men and the materials of war. Big fast ships such as *Kyarra* had an important role to play – and so, once the hostilities began, she was requisitioned by the British government in October 1914. Her hull was painted white, large red crosses were emblazoned on it and she was fitted out as a hospital ship.

On 5 December 1914 she sailed from Australia for the battlegrounds with five fully equipped medical units aboard under the control of Australian officers and crew. She arrived at Alexandretta and hospitals were established at Heliopolis, Zeitun and El Mena. *Kyarra* then returned to Australia carrying wounded troops.

The *Kyarra* subsequently made several trips to Britain carrying cargo and was also involved in the landing of Anzac Expeditionary troops in the Dardanelles. She then went on to make several trips to Britain carrying cargo and returning to Australia for the last time just before Christmas 1917. Commonwealth control of her then ended on 4 January 1918. On 19 January 1918, Captain Albert Donovan took command of the *Kyarra* from her previous captain, W. Smith, and she was readied to return once again to Britain.

Kyarra sailed from Melbourne on 8 February 1918, calling at Wellington, New Zealand, before crossing the Pacific and arriving at Bilboa at the Panama Canal on 18 March. Passing through the Canal, she made her way up the east coast of America before heading out across the open waters of the Atlantic for the European war zone.

Kyarra arrived in London safely in early May 1918, where lading started of 2,500 tons of general cargo to be shipped back to Australia along with the war wounded. She was subsequently to embark at Devonport, Plymouth, towards the south-west end of the English Channel. Little did Captain Donovan or his industrious crew know that *Kyarra* would never complete the return journey, for her path was shortly to cross that of Oberleutnant Johannes Lohs, a U-boat 'ace', with more than 100,000 tons of Allied shipping sunk to his name.

On the evening of 22 May Oberleutnant Lohs, in command of *UB-57* of the Flanders Flotilla, had taken the U-boat out of its base at Zeebruge. He had successfully passed on the surface under cover of darkness over the Belgian coastal barrage, a wall of nets and mines. He had then run the Dover net barrage which ran from the Goodwins to the Snou Bank. After that it was the feared wall of nets, mines, sound detector loops and patrol vessels that formed an almost impenetrable barrier right the way across the Channel from Folkestone to Cap Gris Nez.

Having safely broken through these defences into the wider expanses of the Channel, in the early hours of 23 May he moved quietly to take up a waiting position on the surface not far from the Owers Lightship. Invisible in the darkness, he waited for his prey to come to him.

Lohs was alerted by the watch to an approaching convoy of five merchant vessels and naval escort vessels. Springing into action, Lohs had *UB-57* stalk the convoy. Then, just before dawn, *UB-57* successfully torpedoed and sunk the troopship *Moldavia* with the loss of 56 American servicemen (see Chapter Eight). Despite frantic depth-charging by the naval escort vessels, Lohs was able to slip away unseen from his pursuers to continue his patrol. It was with this sinking that Lohs acquired the title 'ace' for having sunk 100,000 tons of Allied shipping.

The following day, 24 May 1918, the SS *Kyarra* had sailed from Tilbury bound for Australia. Captain Donovan's orders were to proceed to Devonport, Plymouth, towards the western end of the Channel where 1,000 wounded and disabled Australian troops would be embarked for onward repatriation to Australia. The *Kyarra*'s holds were already filled with her 2,500 tons of general cargo which included bales of silk, linoleum, French perfume, beer bottles, champagne, perfume, vinegar, Worcester sauce, watches, crockery, sealing wax, lotions and medical supplies.

In good conditions the *Kyarra* had left Tilbury and turned into the Channel. Running down the Channel, Dover, Eastbourne and Brighton all hove into view on her starboard side before slipping astern of her.

As the early dawn of 26 May lightened the skies, the Isle of Wight passed by on her starboard side, to her north. Captain Donovan, obeying his orders, commanded that a zig-zag course be steered and that a look out be posted all round.

On passing St Catherine's Point, the very southern tip of the Isle of Wight, *Kyarra*'s course was altered to the north-west to keep her close into the shore. As the Needles was approached Captain Donovan made a further change of course to take *Kyarra* close inshore into Poole Bay towards the lighthouse at Anvil Point, near Swanage.

At a speed of 12.5 knots and under the charge of the Channel Pilot *Kyarra* had started to move round Anvil Point, about a mile to the south of it. But, hidden in the seas here lay Oberleutnant Lohs and *UB-57*. Lohs was able to identify his prey and take up a perfect firing position to the south of her which allowed an escape route to the open expanses and deeper water of the Channel.

At 8.50 a.m. Lohs gave the firing command and a bow torpedo was loosed. The torpedo ran straight and true towards the port side of the unsuspecting *Kyarra*.

On the *Kyarra* the ordinary hubbub and routine of shipboard life was suddenly shattered as one of the lookouts shouted 'Torpedo approaching on the port side.'

Captain Donovan ran over to the port side of the bridge and saw the tell-tale track of the torpedo approaching about 70 yards away. He immediately ordered the helm hard-a-port – but before the ship had had time to answer to the helm, the torpedo struck the *Kyarra*. The fatal and devastating impact wounded *Kyarra* amidships on the port side in the vicinity of the engine-room, just forward of the boilers. Five of her crew were killed instantly by the explosion. *Kyarra*'s hull was rent open to the sea and tons of cold dark water started flooding into her. Almost immediately, her trim was altered and she started to settle by the bow. Her engines were put out of action instantly and she slewed to a wallowing stop. The order to abandon ship was given and the lifeboats were winched down from their davits atop the midships superstructure.

The rate of the *Kyarra*'s settling into the sea accelerated. Her decks began to slope down towards the bow. As water flooded her forward sections the bow section lost its buoyancy and started to disappear beneath the sea, dragging the rest of the ship with it. Sea water rushed throughout the open spaces of the hull, forcing air out. The water level crept up her foredeck and as the bow section tried to sink to the seabed, slowly at first, her stern started to rise up out of the water.

Twenty minutes after the torpedo strike the *Kyarra* started her final plunge into the depths. As the waters closed over her stern she disappeared from sight and plunged downwards through 30 metres of water. In just a matter of seconds her descent from the surface was over and she careered into the seabed. The *Kyarra* had found her last resting place. A count of heads in the lifeboats revealed the loss of the five crew members who had been in the engine-room at the time of the explosion. One of the men in the boats was also found to be in a very bad state and died from his injuries soon after landing at Swanage.

As the waters closed over her, the *Kyarra* was largely forgotten about – just one of countless wrecks, the legacy of a cruel war of attrition. Not worthy of salvage and not presenting a danger to shipping she was left to lie in peace as the Great War moved on to its inescapable conclusion.

The wreck soon became colonised by fish and sea creatures, grateful of this new shelter in their domain. Ironically, despite the tragic circumstances of her loss on the surface, down in the depths the *Kyarra* became a living reef, a welcome home to myriad types of sealife, known only to humankind amongst local fisherman as an obstruction. As the human memories of her story passed with the years she was forgotten about – until the start of the modern boom in scuba diving in the 1960s.

After sinking the *Kyarra*, Oberleutnant Lohs took *UB-57* stealthily away from the scene. After sinking several small ships including three French sailing vessels he attacked the *War Panther* and *Galileo*, hitting both with torpedoes. Both vessels were however saved by beaching. He was able safely to return to Zeebruge on 1 June.

Loh's career as an ace would not last long. He would go on to sink some 150,000 tons of Allied shipping comprising 76 merchant vessels of varying sizes and a warship. But just three months after sinking the *Kyarra*, in August 1918, only a few months before the Armistice would halt the fighting in November 1918, he lost his life when the U-boat he was in command of struck a mine on a return trip to Germany.

In all, six of the crew of the *Kyarra* died in the attack by *UB-57*: J. Brown, H.G.W. Morley, D. McKenzie, J.A. Nanless, L.A. McPhun and W. Small. Their names are recorded on the Australian Merchant Seamen's Memorial in Campbell, a suburb of Canberra in the Australian Capital Territory. The memorial is formed around the central block of three large concrete and stone structures in the Sculpture Garden on the west side of the main Memorial Building. The north and south sides of the block carry plaques recording the names and ships of the Australian merchant seamen who died during the First and Second World Wars. On the west side of the block there is a poignant bronze sculpture, *Survivors*, designed by Dennis Adams, a war artist during the Second World War, which depicts seamen who have survived a sinking helping others into a rubber liferaft.

The wreck of the *Kyarra*, although known to local fishermen, was discovered for sport diving in 1966 by the Kingston and Elmbridge branch of the BSAC who went on to buy the wreck. She has been regularly dived ever since and has become Dorset's most dived wreck. Although her remains lie in a tidal area which makes diving her at slack water essential, it is common to find many dive boats and RIBs, congregating above her remains in the run-up to slack water, waiting for the tide to ease, allowing divers to descend through the gloom to visit her remains.

Today the wreck of the *Kyarra* lies in about 30 metres of water a short boat ride out of Swanage. She is such a popular wreck dive that a number of hard boats run regular shuttle-runs out to her in time for slack water from both Swanage and Poole. From Swanage it is only a short, leisurely hard boat ride of about 20 minutes out to the site.

The wreck lies orientated north-east/south-west with her bows to the north-east. She lies on her starboard side and is in quite an advanced state of collapse although she still retains her basic ship shape. The collapsing means that many large pieces of ship's machinery and gear, normally hidden from view, are open and accessible. Add to that the fact that the wreck is heavily colonised by sealife and you start to see the *Kyarra*'s attraction. Schools of fish drift over her remains whilst velvet swimming crabs, lobsters and squat lobsters inhabit her nooks and crannies, and the rocky ledges and outcrops around. Sponges and soft corals such as 'Dead Men's Fingers' festoon the wreck, giving her an eerie, ghost-like feel.

DIVE DETAILS FOR THE WRECK OF THE SS *KYARRA*

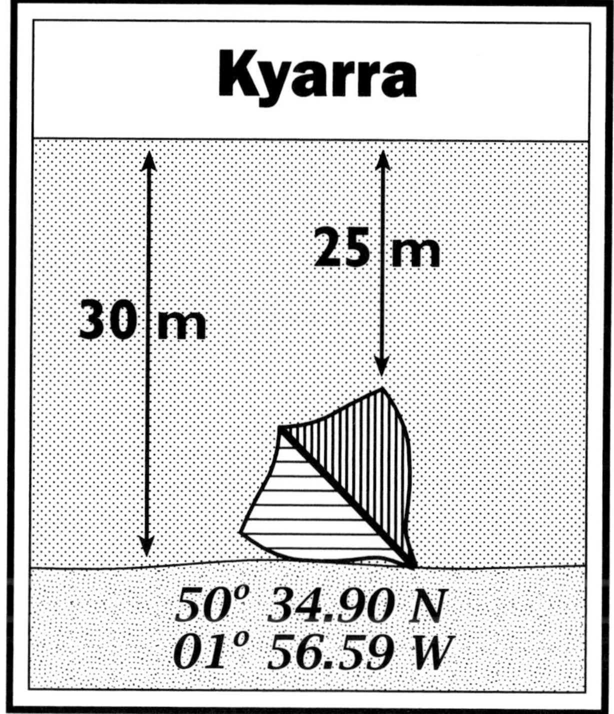

The most easily recognisable section of the *Kyarra* is her stern, which retains its basic shape. The stern section is one of the few places where the orientation of the wreck on the seabed can be made out easily. On the stern post itself the pintles (large upright pins) on which the rudder was formerly mounted via its corresponding fixing rings known as gudgeons can be made out, the top one would have been above the water level. The orientation of the stern reveals that the wreck is canted over by 70–80 degrees. On the seabed here lies the rudder, fallen from its mounts, its gudgeons still seemingly ready to accept the weight of the rudder once again.

The free section of uppermost port-side propellor shaft where it protrudes from the hull can be made out above, still fixed in place by its A bracket. Inboard the massive steering quadrant can be made out amongst a jumble of debris, with two sets of steering gear winches and two sets of mooring bollards collapsed down into the innards of the ship.

THE WRECK OF THE ONCE-BEAUTIFUL SS *KYARRA*

Moving forward from the stern, the uppermost port side of the hull retains its shape at first. Here rows of portholes allow shafts of light to penetrate into the dark cavernous sections of her interior. An open doorway in the hull allows easy access to this area. The deeper starboard side of the hull here is more broken up and pieces of her original plating and her ribs stick up from the seabed here and there.

Further forward, the uppermost port side of the hull has rotted away to expose the portside crankshaft and thrust bearings that held the prop in place and stopped it screwing itself into the hull. Further forward still, the uppermost port side of the hull shows the damage caused by the fatal torpedo explosion. This is the area of the engine-room and the *Kyarra*'s large boilers can be made out here, partly obscured by fallen plating. Of the *Kyarra*'s large central superstructure which ran from aft of the engine-room forward to the bridge itself, there is now no trace. On the seabed below a donkey boiler can be seen, fallen out of the wreck itself.

Moving forward beyond the engine-room the wreck

itself becomes confused and difficult to follow at first. A section of her large funnel, now collapsed and partly covered by plating, can be made out. The large bridge superstructure which formerly stood atop here is long gone and now we are left with a jumble of collapsed sections of plating, the remnants of her interior structure and some girders sticking out.

Forward, beyond the area of her vanished bridge, the remains of her collapsed foredeck are of much interest, the cargo hatches discernable in the debris. A section of her tubular foremast runs out from the hull onto the seabed. On the deeper starboard side of the hull, jagged sections of plating and girders jut up, a legacy of where the deck once was fixed before its inward and downward collapse.

Beyond Hatch No. 1 the anchor winch sits in the debris athwartships. At either side of the hull here, two sets of twin mooring bollards can be made out in the tumbled debris. The anchor chains run out from the winch forward but the hull suddenly and abruptly is cut short before the bow itself at the collision bulkhead. A catastrophic event has happened here which has sheared off the very bow section. We are now faced with the

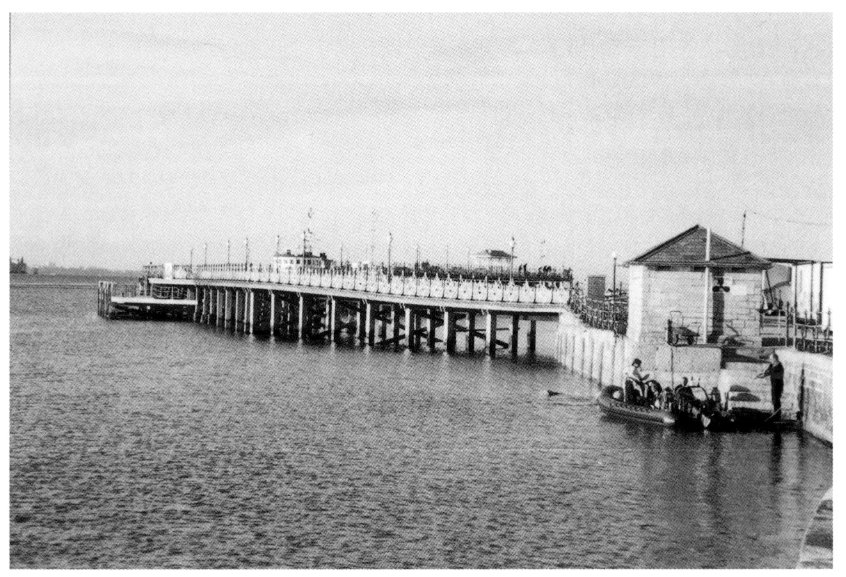

THE PICTURESQUE PIER AT SWANAGE FROM WHERE REGULAR DIVE BOAT SHUTTLES OUT TO THE *KYARRA* DEPART.
PHOTO: AUTHOR'S COLLECTION

detached chain locker and a large rectangular section of the bow itself.

Many hard boats depart from the picturesque pier at Swanage for the wreck site. The short journey out follows the coastline with its cliffs, rocky outcrops and beautiful scenery ashore. Swanage itself is a delightful small town which has not lost its identity and been engulfed by modern developments. It has a fantastic atmosphere and I enjoyed my time there.

Swanage has become something of a centre for diving and in addition to the hard boats operating in the area, RIBs full of divers are a common sight in and around the harbour. The pier itself makes a very interesting and atmospheric shore dive and night dive.

There is a small car-parking area right at the pier itself, and convenient trolleys laid on to push your heavy kit the length of the pier to the landing jetty. There is also a dive shop and air station on site at the pier. Swanage holds much of interest for the diver, in addition to having one of England's greatest wrecks on its doorstep.

Essential Information

BOAT LAUNCH SITE: Several hard boats run regular shuttles out from the closest port, Swanage, to the wreck to coincide with slack water. Boats presently operating include *Sidewinder* (01929) 427064, Divers Down 7.5m RIB, *Okenos* (01929) 423565, *Beowulf* (01202) 697844 and *Swanage Diver* (07977) 142661. It is a pleasant short ride of a few miles out to the site, 20–25 minutes away. RIBs can be launched at Swanage and more distant Poole, about ten miles away.

TIDAL CONDITIONS: Strongly tidal area – this wreck *must* be dived at slack water. Very short slack at springs with tide turning quickly.

VISIBILITY: Visibility varies greatly. On some occasions it can be a silty 3m, at other times 5–10m.

MAXIMUM DEPTH: 30msw.

LEAST DEPTH: 25msw.

COASTGUARD: Portland and Weymouth Coastguard (01305) 760439.

RECOMPRESSION FACILITIES: Poole Hyperbaric Hotline (01426) 316636. Institute of Naval Medicine Gosport Hotline (07831) 151523.

AIR SUPPLIES: Divers Down, The Pier, Swanage (01929) 423565, Dorset Diving Services, Units 6 and 7 Elliot Road, West Howe Ind. Estate, Bournemouth (01202) 580065, Forward Diving Services, Unit M, Arthur Brays Yard, West Quay Rd, Poole (01202) 677128, Diving Leisure Unlimited, Rockley Park, Hamworthy, Poole (01202) 718522.

HYDROGRAPHIC CHART: Bill of Portland to The Needles, No. 2615.

POSITION: Lat 50 34.90 N, Long 001 56.59 W.

DIVER LEVEL: *Kyarra* is a safe wreck dive but is in a general depth of 25–30msw. It therefore makes an ideal first wreck dive for progressing divers but is not suitable for novices because of the depth.

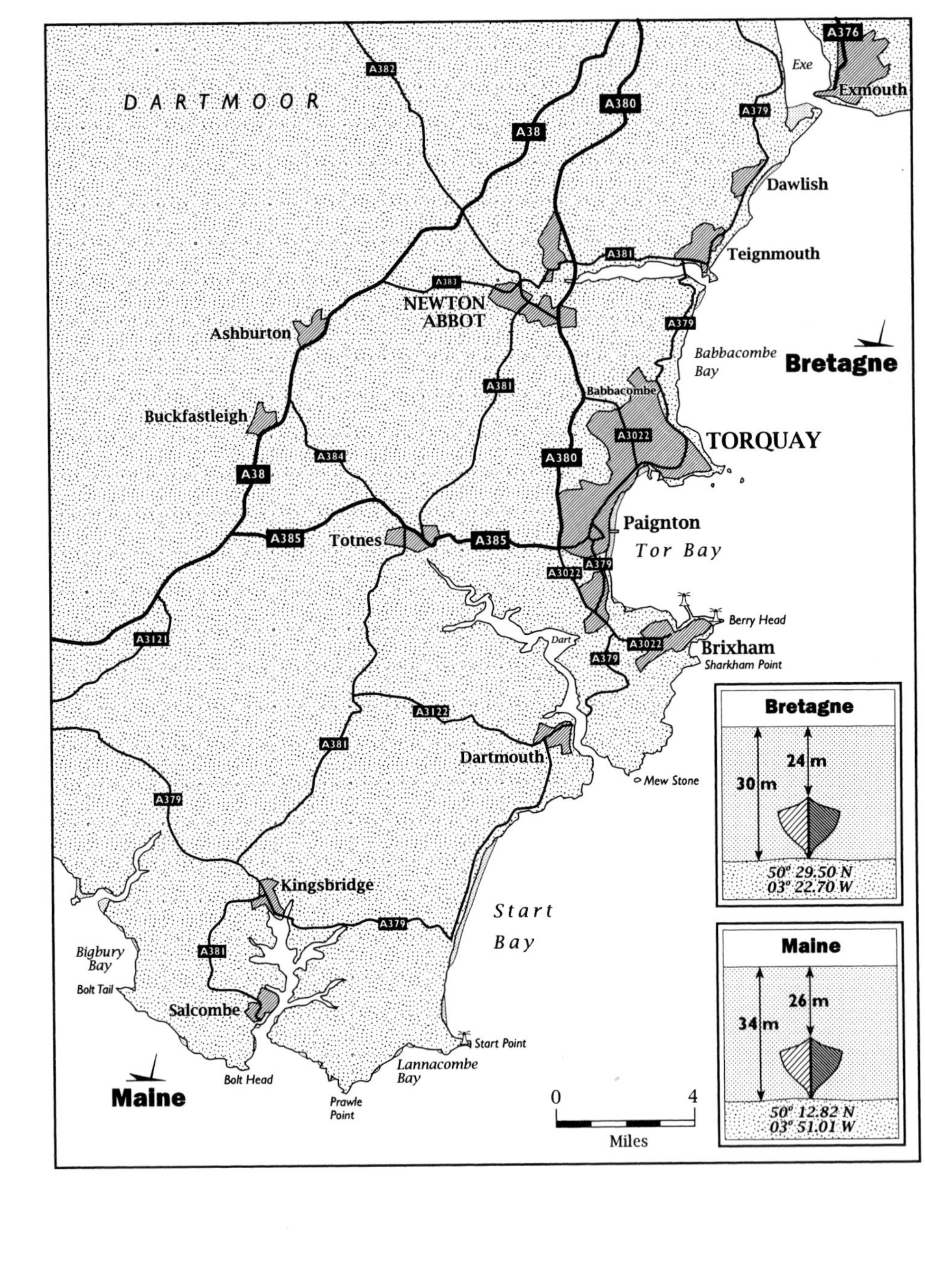

DARTMOOR
A382
A380
A38
A376
Exe
Exmouth
A379
Dawlish
Teignmouth
A381
A383
NEWTON ABBOT
Ashburton
A379
Babbacombe Bay
Bretagne
A381
Babbacombe
Buckfastleigh
A3022
TORQUAY
A384
A380
A38
Paignton
A385
Totnes
A385
Tor Bay
A379
A3022
A3121
Berry Head
Dart
A3022
Brixham
A379
Sharkham Point
A3122
A381
Dartmouth
Mew Stone
A379
Kingsbridge
A379
Start Bay
Bigbury Bay
A381
Bolt Tail
Salcombe
Start Point
Lannacombe Bay
Bolt Head
Prawle Point
Maine
0
4
Miles
Bretagne
24 m
30 m
50° 29.50 N
03° 22.70 W
Maine
26 m
34 m
50° 12.82 N
03° 51.01 W

Chapter 5

SS *Maine*, Salcombe, South Devon

The 3,616 gross tons SS *Maine* was laid down in 1904 at the D. & W. Henderson, Shipbuilders, yard in Partick, Scotland. Starting life humbly as Job No. 440, she was commissioned with this long-established shipbuilding firm by the Sierra Shipping Company of Liverpool.

D. & W. Henderson themselves had initially been founded as a marine engineering venture by David and William Henderson, two of four brothers in the 1850s. Another brother, Thomas, was responsible for founding the Anchor Line in Glasgow in 1856. In the mid-1860s D. & W. Henderson purchased the defunct shipbuilding yard of Tod & MacGregor at Partick, and their business went from strength to strength in the great era of shipbuilding. Eventually the firm was bought by Harland & Wolf (famed builders of the *Titanic*) of Belfast in 1917.

The hull of Job 440 was launched in January 1905 and she was completed in July that year. She was given the official number 120821 and was named *Sierra Blanca*. The newly christened ship was 375 feet in length, with a beam of 46 feet. The *Sierra Blanca* was constructed in the traditional and classic way of a cargo workhorse of her time – straight stem, cavernous foredeck holds, bridge superstructure amidships with a single-storey deckhouse behind above the engine-room. Aft of the engine- and boiler-rooms, and superstructure above, lay more cargo

OPPPOSITE: LOCATION CHART FOR WRECKS OF THE SS *MAINE* AND SS *BRETAGNE*.

holds. She was a functional, well-designed cargo ship, built for hauling substantial cargoes around the seas.

In 1913 she was bought for £38,500 by the Atlantic Transport Company who renamed her *Maine*. She would sail the seas under this name for only a further four short years until dawn on 23 March 1917, when she would be sent to the bottom, another victim of an unseen U-boat, *UC-17*. Today she is one of the finest dives in the South Devon area, attracting hundreds of divers to her each year. The wreck is owned by the Torbay branch of the British Sub-Aqua Club (BSAC).

UC-17 – THE PATROL

17 March 1917: The small U-boat *UC-17*, under the command of Oberleutnant Ralph Wenniger, slips out of Zeebruge in the safety of the darkness of the early hours. She is loaded with seven torpedoes and a complement of mines with orders to proceed to Beachy Head and thereafter to Newhaven to lay mine barrages to sink shipping. After initially running on the surface Oberleutnant Wenniger submerges *UC-17*, runs down the English Channel underwater and successfully lays mines at Beachy Head.

19 March: Two days after leaving Zeebruge, UC-17 surfaces close to the small French fishing vessel *Rhodora*. A boarding party opens her seacocks and sends her to the bottom. In London's East India Dock, the Atlantic Transport Company's 3,616-ton steamship SS *Maine* is nearing the end of lading. In her holds is a small and hardly profitable cargo of 500 tons of chalk and 50 tons of general stores. She is bound to leave London in two days' time for Philadelphia where, once her outbound cargo is offloaded, her holds would be filled to the brim with very valuable war supplies for the continuing conflict in Europe.

21 March: After moving to Newhaven and laying a mine barrage there, *UC-17* moves further down the Channel, heading towards Start Point. On the way she encounters the 51-ton English fishing vessel *Curlew*, which is also sent to the bottom by a boarding party, this time by planting grenades. The same day *UC-17* stalks the 2,933-ton steamer *Huntscape* but a bow shot from *UC-17* misses her and she escapes unharmed. At 9 a.m. the steamship *Maine*'s mooring ropes are cast off and she slips out of the East India Dock for the long voyage across the Atlantic. Unknown to her *UC-17* is at work in the Channel, scouring the seas for further prey.

22 March: Twenty-four miles to the east of Start Point, *UC-17* encounters the immense and beautiful 11,130-ton New Zealand Shipping Company steamship SS *Rotorua* en route from Wellington, New Zealand, via Newport News bound for London with a valuable cargo of 5,600 tons of general New Zealand goods. Wenniger made no mistake this time with such a large prize. One of his seven

THE BEAUTIFUL 11,130-TON NEW ZEALAND SHIPPING CO. STEAMSHIP *ROTORUA* WAS SUNK BY *UC-17* THE DAY BEFORE SHE SANK THE SS *MAINE*.
PHOTO COURTESY OF THE NATIONAL MARITIME MUSEUM, GREENWICH

torpedoes was loosed and ran straight and true blasting into the *Rotorua* and killing one seaman aboard her. Such a large ship took enough time to sink to allow her crew to safely abandon ship into the lifeboats. The loss of the *Rotorua* pushed Britain's losses that March to beyond 100 ships, a monthly record for the war.

23 March: The cold late-March dawn cast its weak light onto grey seas revealing the *Maine*, well down the Channel, about 13 miles south of Berry Head. The fear of a U-boat attack gripped all aboard the *Maine*. The crew knew that they were now well and truly in the U-boat killing grounds. They were all too aware that ships were being sunk at an alarming rate by the unseen U-boat menace. They had no doubt learned of the fate of the *Rotorua* and were aware that a U-boat was active. If only they could slip through the Channel unscathed and break into the Atlantic they would be relatively safe from further attack.

Special lookouts had been placed at the f'c'stle, at the very bow of the ship and at the stern. As the crew had breakfast and went about their duties the lookouts peered out at the seas around them, straining their eyes, continuously searching for the feared tell-tale wake of a periscope or the track of a torpedo. The cold, damp, salt-laden air gnawed at their bones, chilling their skin, seemingly sucking the heat from their bodies.

The *Maine* was zigzagging in an attempt to confuse any

U-boat predator with its sudden turns to port or starboard. Although the seas were short, rain squalls whipped across the seas from time to time, temporarily obscuring visibility. The crew were unaware that they were being stalked by *UC-17* and Oberleutnant Wenniger.

At 8.05 a.m., after studying the progress and course of the *Maine* through his periscope, Oberleutnant Wenniger brought his U-boat into an attack profile and gave the order to fire. His torpedo ran straight and true towards the unsuspecting steamship.

All the precautions taken by the *Maine* had failed. Neither the tracking periscope nor the run of the torpedo had been seen by the lookouts, whose job had been made difficult by the sea conditions. The first knowledge of the threat came when an almighty explosion on the port side, just forward of the bridge at No. 2 Hold, rocked the ship to her core. The plume of water from a torpedo strike made it obvious to all instantly what had happened. The covers for Hatches 2 and 3 were blown right off by the expanding force of the explosion. The bridge was partially wrecked, and Captain Johnston was knocked to the deck. With No. 2 Hold rent open to the sea, tons of cold sea water started flooding into the cavernous space, immediately starting to alter her trim. The crew could feel her starting to settle by the head.

Captain Johnston picked himself up from the deck and ordered that the presence of the U-boat be reported by radio and by using rockets. There were also some small vessels in the distance and the message was repeated by flags. He then altered course and started heading for land to try and save his stricken ship. The engine-room had not been affected by the explosion but as No. 2 Hold filled up and she settled deeper into the sea, so the searching water was starting to inexorably make its way through the bowels of the ship.

After she had struggled a dozen miles towards land, the water reached the stokehold and her engines had to be stopped. The *Maine* slowed and wallowed to a halt, rocking gently in the short seas. The seemingly eternal onboard sound of the ship's engines died away to be replaced by the silence of the open sea. The crew didn't know if the U-boat was still in the area. It might have considered its job was finished and left the scene of the attack. Alternatively, it might be shadowing the *Maine*'s progress, watching to see if it was necessary to use another torpedo to finish her off. At any moment there could be another explosion that might violently end the lives of some or all of the crew.

In fact, after watching his torpedo strike what he considered a fatal blow to the *Maine*, knowing he was in dangerous waters, Oberleutnant Wenniger had taken *UC-17* away from the scene of the attack submerged, heading north-east. He was able to make his way back safely to Zeebruge after what had been a very effective patrol.

Back on the *Maine* however, Captain Johnston gave the order for a lifeboat to be lowered but as this was happening a naval torpedo boat, No. 99, under the command of Lieutenant Commander Percy Taylor, DSc, was seen heading towards the stricken vessel. Lieutenant Commander Taylor had been in command of a flotilla of minesweepers clearing mines from the approaches to Dartmouth and Teignmouth and had seen the *Maine* in difficulty. He took his torpedo boat alongside the *Maine* and rescued the crew, including those who had boarded the lifeboat. Captain Johnston, the Chief Officer and the First and Second Officers and a few crew remained aboard the *Maine* to assist in a tow.

Captain Johnston briefed Lieutenant Commander Taylor on the *Maine*'s distress and it was decided to try to tow her and beach her in either Hope Cove or Bigbury Bay. The tow line was rigged and the tow commenced. Lieutenant Commander Taylor radioed Plymouth Command asking for tug assistance.

The tow proved to be very difficult. The *Maine* was a large vessel, she was settled deeply into the water and her big holds were filling with water. The tow was painfully slow – it was like pulling a colossal lead weight. Too much tension too quickly on the tow wire and it would break, unable to cope with the inertia of the stricken hull. Time and again the tow wire parted. Other patrol boats arrived and took tow wires to assist.

At noon, some four hours after the attack, the first tug arrived and a new tow was established. Not long after, however, under the pressure of water inside her one of her internal bulkheads collapsed and what little dry area there was inside became one vast space into which water poured, robbing the *Maine* of her last vestiges of buoyancy.

At 12.45 p.m., upright and on an even keel, the sea finally swallowed the *Maine* some two and a half miles north-west of Bolt Head. There was no final flourish or standing on end for the final plunge into the abyss. She just settled deeper and deeper – and then as the waters closed over her, her captain and remaining crew calmly stepped in to a dingy that had been made ready, and floated off as the ship's deck disappeared beneath their feet.

The *Maine* however was not gone forever without trace. Once she had settled on the bottom it was found that both her 100-feet tall foremast and main mast projected some 12 feet clear of the water at low water. They were an obvious and very dangerous obstruction to any vessels navigating in the area, particularly at High Water, when they would be almost totally submerged but just beneath the surface. This situation led to fairly speedy action being taken to safeguard shipping. Notice to Mariners No. 370 of the year 1917 was issued by the Hydrographic Department of the Admiralty a month later on 2 April 1917 warning seafarers of the danger.

Oberleutnant Wenniger was able to navigate *UC-17* safely back to Zeebruge and continued serving as part of the Flanders Flotilla, constantly having to run the gauntlet of steel anti-submarine nets and mines laid by the British. For his successful command of *UC-17* he was promoted to Kapitänleutnant and given command of a new attack U-boat, *UB-55*, later in 1917. At a time when U-boat losses were high, Wenniger's skill and ability helped him to survive for another year and become a respected veteran of the flotilla. His luck would not last him through the war, though.

In the protective darkness of the night of 22 April 1918, Wenniger was navigating *UB-55* through the Straits of Dover Barrage on the surface. Just as he was nearly through, he was spotted by an armed trawler and several patrolling drifters. Searchlights lit up the darkness and fixed on *UB-55*. Wenniger crash-dived the boat, getting submerged in 30 seconds, but unbeknown to him a wall of steel nets and mines lay in his path and *UB-55* struck a submerged mine. The explosion caused a huge shudder throughout the U-boat and she reeled from the impact.

UB-55's pressure hull had been damaged and water started pouring into her. The lights went out and the crew were plunged into a terrifying darkness. They could feel that *UB-55* had started to drop downwards like a lead weight. The terrified crew waited for what seemed an eternity as she plunged into the dark depths. Finally *UB-55* hit the seabed with a jarring thump.

Freezing water continued pouring into the U-boat and soon it had risen to waist height. Frantically the crew worked to try and regain control of the stricken vessel, but the boat was dead and none of the controls responded. In the darkness Wenniger knew there was only one chance of survival for his men – a free ascent from the conning tower hatch to the surface some 100 feet above. He gathered the crew close around him at the conning tower hatch as the water continued its remorseless rise within the ruptured hull, compressing the remaining air inside.

The crew felt the increasing pressure on their ears and as the air compressed at such speed it became hot and clammy. When the air pressure inside the hull was roughly equal to the water pressure outside it was possible to open the hatch upwards. Wenniger gave the command and the hatch opened upwards easily. The remaining air disappeared immediately from the conning tower, rising upwards. Cold sea water poured with force into the darkness of the hull as the crew struggled to remain in position ready to swim free. In a short space of time, the U-boat was full of water and devoid of air. The crew were terrified, holding their breath as they desperately struggled by touch to find their way up and out through the hatch into free water. It was a slow process for the men to singly exit the U-boat. Some were unable to hold their breath long enough, gulping for air that was not there, their lungs filling with water. Slowly their thrashing struggles subsided, to be replaced by stillness.

Wenniger was one of the last to leave the U-boat. Twenty of the crew of thirty-four managed to get out of the hull. Those unfortunates who did not have time to get out drowned in the terrifying darkness. Of the 20 who managed to escape from the coffin of steel and rise up through the 100 feet of water, only 6, including Wenniger himself, managed to survive. The others perhaps held their breath as they ascended, burst their lungs and lost consciousness – some no doubt could not swim in any event and even if they made the surface were destined to drown. Perhaps others made the surface but were not spotted and drifted away, slowly succumbing to the freezing cold of the March waters and lapsing into unconsciousness.

Wenniger and his five surviving crew were picked up and spent the rest of the war in British prisoner-of-war camps. Wenniger himself was held at a POW camp for officers at Donnington Hall, Leicestershire. He was last heard of as executive officer on the German cruiser *Berlin* in 1929.

Following the War, the *Maine* was wire-swept to bring down her masts, clear her upper superstructure and remove the hazard to shipping. After that she was forgotten about, just one of thousands of war losses around Britain's shores. She had a very poor cargo for her outward journey to America, just chalk and general stores. Certainly she held nothing of any worth that would merit the costs of a salvage operation.

After the war there was such an abundance of scrap metal in the form of armaments, shell casings and the like, that the price of non-ferrous material was very low. It was so low that even though her masts initially still projected from the sea marking her resting place, even her 6-ton bronze propellor, which could be fairly easily recovered, was not an attractive commercial salvage proposition. And so, once her masts came down, memory of the *Maine*, her whereabouts and her story gradually faded, with the passing of the years, from human memory. Eventually her identity was lost and the only people who knew of her existence were the local fishermen in the area. She became known only as the 'Railway-line Wreck', an interesting and seemingly inappropriate name for her, given her cargo. Perhaps the name referred to a land point or transit that the fishermen used to fix her position in the days long before modern navigational instruments.

In 1961 divers from the Torbay branch of the BSAC were the first divers to dive down to this mystery wreck. They reported that she was a steamship sitting on an even keel, relatively intact barring some of her superstructure lying on the

THE WRECK OF THE SS *MAINE*, OFF BOLT HEAD, SOUTH DEVON. © ROD MACDONALD 2003

seabed beside her – presumably as a result of post-war clearance work on her. That year the club dived on the wreck many times and established its identity. Subsequently a salvage syndicate from the club was formed with shares being sold at £5 each. Once sufficient funds had been raised they went on to buy the wreck from the Liverpool underwriters for £100.

The four-bladed propeller, some 17 feet across, now became the focus of their attention. On the prop they found the manufacturer's name, 'Stone's Bronze', its year of manufacture, 1904, and the job no., 440. The manufacturers were tracked down and offered to buy back the prop from the syndicate at £137 per ton. The divers were able to successfully blast the prop off the wreck in one piece and using an Admiralty mooring vessel with its bow winch, the *Barbastel*, were able to recover the prop for collection at Devonport by Stone's.

In 1983 the ferrous spare cast-iron propeller was raised and became a feature at the then new Victoria Shopping Centre in Paignton. The bell was only discovered in 1987, despite the many hundreds of dives on it since the vessel's rediscovery for sport diving. The bell was lying nearly totally covered up at the bottom of a hole near the forward deck anchor winches.

Today the wreck of the *Maine* is not as well known and dived as it should be. For me, having spent some time diving the greatest wrecks in England whilst researching this book, I found the *Maine* to be up there ranking as one of the greatest. A combination of its location and strong local tides make this wreck one that has to be finely judged and dived at slack water. If conditions are right, the *Maine* will surprise and delight you.

The *Maine* lies on a clean white sand and shale seabed at a depth of 32–34 metres. She lies about two nautical miles south-south-east of Bolt Tail and two and a half nautical miles north-west of Bolt Head. Located offshore from these headlands, strong currents keep this area clean of any silt or sediment that would cloud visibility. Consequently, it is not uncommon to have underwater visibility of 20–30 metres, exceptional for this close inshore in the Channel.

The wreck sits on an even keel more or less in a north/south direction, with her bows pointing in towards the shore. The least depth to her main deck is about 26 metres. It is clear that the *Maine* is collapsing downwards as most of her upper main deck has already done so and now sits on her shelter deck, a deck level below. Main deck fitments such as anchor winches and bollards still sit upright in their correct locations, simply one deck or more below where they formerly stood. The very distinctive straight narrow stem at the bow makes a majestic sight.

After the torpedo struck, Captain Johnston had turned the *Maine* and made a desperate dash towards shore, hoping to beach her before she sank. Although water was flooding into her, the engines were not affected initially by the explosion. The *Maine* laboured towards shore for about a dozen miles before the volume of inrushing water overwhelmed the engines and she wallowed to a stop. The ensuing frantic attempt to tow the *Maine* to safety failed and she eventually succumbed to the seas. Her bows still head in hope of salvation towards shore, a silent testimony to that fateful and futile dash for shallow water to beach her.

The *Maine*'s straight and seemingly sharp stem is an imposing sight, dropping down into the shadowy gloom below. Both her port- and starboard-side anchors remain neatly stowed away in their hawse pipes.

Up on the f'c'stle deck, the decking has collapsed downwards into the bowels of the ship leaving a large open void. The only identifying item to mark the end of the f'c'stle is a single spar running athwartships at roof level where the bulkhead would have been. All the items normally found up on top of the f'c'stle deck are now to be found several decks down inside the ship. At the bottom of the f'c'stle can be found two sets of twin mooring bollards, dotted either side of the deck. Behind them the large anchor winch, with its chains run out to the anchor hawses, is also in situ, but collapsed down through several decks to the bottom of the f'c'stle.

Aft of the f'c'stle void, Hold No. 1 can be explored, the top being at shelter deck level. The sides of the ship rise up on either side, giving protection from any current there may be. The collapse here of the main deck has left jagged struts and spars sticking up at main deck level. Either side of the hatch opening, the decking has rotted away to reveal the beams and frame of her decking.

Moving aft, Hold No. 2 is at first seemingly open for inspection. Its hatch is still discernible at shelter deck level, the sides of the ship rearing up to main deck level. However, the aft end of this hold has been completely opened up. This is where the fateful torpedo struck on the port side. The hull of the ship drops away virtually to the seabed at both sides. The catastrophic effects of the single torpedo explosion are quite visible – the blow must have torn the heart out of the ship.

Aft of the torpedo damage the hull seems to reform again towards where the bridge superstructure would have originally stood – but it soon becomes clear that the hull just rises to the level of the engine-room deep within the bowels of the ship. It is as though the entire superstructure has been detached and removed. Perhaps this was during the post-war wire sweep. Alternatively, perhaps the superstructure was blown and lifted off by a grab. Either way, it probably lies close by. This was a common way for salvers to get access to the valuable non-ferrous metals in the engine-rooms of wrecked ships, a sight familiar to divers on wrecks all around the British coastline.

Three massive boilers are now exposed to view. One is set forward on the centre line of the ship. The two others are set behind it on either side of the hull. Behind the boiler-room, the engine-room is also opened up and easily explored. The large triple-expansion engine sits on the centre line of the vessel, running fore and aft. The drive shaft for her single prop can be made out at the bottom of the engine on the starboard side.

Aft of the engine-room, the sides of the hull rise upwards as the ship regains its original form. There are two after-deck holds. A small cargo winch sits forward of the first whilst another larger winch sits fore and aft on the port side. Either side of the hatch, the decking has rotted away to reveal the transverse beams of her framing.

Between the two after-deck hatches, larger cargo winches sit either side of the stump of the main mast. The mast itself was brought down in the wire sweep and part of it now lies diagonally across the hatch to the aftmost hold. Immediately behind this hold stand the remains of the stern accommodation deckhouse. The lightweight steel of this deckhouse has rotted and disappeared, leaving only a collapsed jumble of struts and spars. Moving further aft, bollards and cleats dot the sides of the hull, but then abruptly the decking ends. Either side there are the tangled struts and spars of the hull itself. Dropping over the side towards the seabed it becomes clear that a large strip of the upper works of the stern deckhouse has peeled away and fallen over the stern of the ship. A large circular platform, perhaps the gun platform, lies upside down on the seabed here, partially obscuring the rudder.

As you would expect in a vessel of this size the rudder and keel of this ship are immense and give a real sense of perspective. The glorious visibility means that divers can take in large sections of this vast wreck at any one time, which helps in orientation on the wreck and understanding its layout. With the clean white sand and spectacular visibility, I found the wreck very reminiscent of diving the Burra

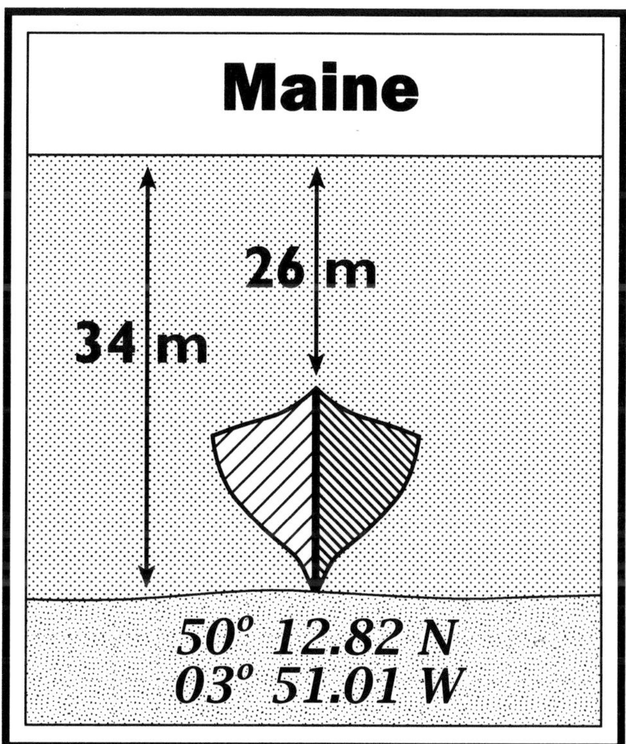

DIVE DETAILS FOR THE 3,616-TON SS *MAINE*

Sound blockships at Scapa Flow, which are renowned for their good visibility.

The *Maine* is so big that it takes several dives to get to know it fully. Once familiar with its layout, divers can return to spend whole dives exploring just one section of it in depth. It is also not too deep a wreck to get good bottom times on it. The *Maine* is also at a depth where Nitrox will be valuable for extending bottom times, shortening any decompression stops and helping to avoid any decompression problems.

Essential Information

BOAT LAUNCH SITE: Small boats and inflatables can be launched from Salcombe.

HARD BOAT DIVING: Hard boats can be chartered from Salcombe and from Plymouth, 12.5 nautical miles away from the site.

TIDAL CONDITIONS: Strongly tidal site. Should be dived at slack water only. Two hours after high water or 2.5 hours after low water.

VISIBILITY: Extremely good. Summer months, 20–30 metres

MAXIMUM DEPTH: 32–34msw.

LEAST DEPTH: 26msw.

COASTGUARD: Brixham Coastguard (01803) 882704.

RECOMPRESSION FACILITIES: DDRC (Diving Diseases Research Centre) (01752) 209999.

AIR SUPPLIES: Deep Blue Diving, The Mountbatten Centre, Plymouth. Air to 320 Bar, Nitrox, including premixed EAN32 and Trimix.

HYDROGRAPHIC CHART: Plymouth to Salcombe, No. 5602.4.

POSITION: Lat 50 12.824 N, Long 003 51.006 W.

DIVER LEVEL: Given the depth and strong currents, this wreck is for experienced divers only.

Chapter 6

SS *Bretagne*, Babbacombe Bay, East Devon

The schooner-rigged single-screw steamer *Bretagne* was built in 1903 by Nylands,Vaerksted in the Norwegian city then known as Christiania but now known as Oslo. She measured 231.6 feet in length, with a beam of 35.2 feet and a draught of 14.7 feet. The *Bretagne* weighed in at 1,382 tons gross, with an under deck of 1,305 tons and net 860 tons. She was constructed with one deck and a spar deck. A triple-expansion engine made by Nylands was fitted to her that could develop 106nhp. In addition to this, she could fly up to 2,000 square feet of sail from her two masts if needed, to increase her speed in favourable conditions or should her engine be put out of action.

THE MAJESTIC SCHOONER-RIGGED SS *BRETAGNE*. PHOTO COURTESY OF STEWART BUTTERFIELD AND THE BRISTOL AEROSPACE SUB-AQUA CLUB

The *Bretagne* was constructed in the classic build of her time, with her engine and boiler-rooms amidships, and the main superstructure housing accommodation and the bridge itself above. Deep cargo holds were set fore and aft of the central superstructure, with two hatches on the foredeck and one aft. Winches were set on the deck around the foremast and main mast to work the cargo derricks. A spare prop was lashed to the deck at the very stern so that it was close to hand should it require to be fitted in the event of damage to the main prop itself.

Either side of the superstructure, coal shutes were set in the deck for loading coal into her bunkers to feed the boilers. At the bow itself, anchor chains rose up from the chain locker below to a sturdy anchor winch set on the deck. From there, twin anchor chains led out to the anchors themselves, one on either side at the bow.

The *Bretagne* was Norwegian-built and initially Norwegian-owned. For the first ten years of her life she served as a general workhorse, ferrying cargoes successfully from port to port. Europe itself however was soon to be consumed by the Great War, the war that would do so much to shape the destiny of Europe. It would also mould the destiny of the *Bretagne* herself.

Initially the *Bretagne* escaped an active war role, but in 1916 she was requisitioned by the Ministry of War Transport and fitted out with a stern defensive 12-pound gun. These stern defensive guns were fitted to merchant vessels once it became clear that U-boats were targeting unarmed vessels. They were designed to allow ships to fire on enemy threats such as U-boats whilst using their greater speed to make good an escape. The *Bretagne* would survive two years of the Great War after her 1916 requisition before meeting her fate, with her stern gun never having been fired in anger.

In August 1918, just three months before the Armistice would silence the guns of the greatest carnage that had ever unfolded across Europe, the *Bretagne* set off, laden with 2000 tons of Welsh steam coal, from Barry in South Glamorgan, Wales, bound for the port of Rouen in France. Her planned route would take her around the south-western tip of England, across the English Channel with Cherbourg eventually passing by on her starboard beam. She would then enter the Baie de la Seine and after Le Havre had passed by on her port side, the *Bretagne* would enter the River Seine itself and proceed up the river to her final destination, the port of Rouen, which is located nearly 35 miles upstream. This small compact steamer, with its shallow draught, would be ideally suited to carry her valuable cargo of coal upstream for offloading at Rouen.

The *Bretagne*'s mooring ropes were cast off at Barry and she and her crew of 19 carefully nudged out of her berth and left the port, heading out into the deeper water of the Bristol Channel. The *Bretagne* then made her way down the north-west coast of the Devon and Cornwall peninsula before rounding Land's End and the Scilly Isles, and heading eastwards into the English Channel. Lizard Point slipped past on her port beam and she headed towards Start Point and Lyme Bay.

On Saturday, 10 August, however, her progress was slowed by thick fog. She had managed to make her way to a position six miles off Berry Head, which is near Torbay on the westernmost side of Lyme Bay.

In those days there were no electronic navigation instruments, so navigating, even just remaining stationary, in thick fog was very dangerous. From the open bridge eyes would have peered into the fog and ears strained to hear the warning noise of another vessel's engines. At the f'c'stle crewmen would have been on watch, alert for any sign of danger and ready to ring out a warning on the f'c'stle bell. Every two minutes a long blast on her steam whistle would be sounded to warn other vessels that she was underway in this restricted visibility.

Suddenly, at about 10.30 a.m., the bows of the French steamship *Renée Marthe* loomed out of the fog bearing down on the *Bretagne*. In the poor visibility, Captain J.W. Johannesson on the *Bretagne* was given little time to react. The bows of the *Renée Marthe* struck the *Bretagne* on the starboard aft quarter, slicing into her hull in the vicinity of the aftmost hold. The noise of the collision, of steel impacting on steel and being rent apart, was so loud that it was heard by the Torbay Boom Defence Vessel which set off to the scene to investigate.

As the *Renée Marthe* pulled away from the *Bretagne* she unplugged the gap and tons of cold dark water started flooding into the *Bretagne*'s hull. Her steering was jammed to starboard and this made it impossible to steer her towards shore and safety – she could not move forward in a straight line. It soon became clear that the hole in her stern was a fatal wound, as despite the efforts of her crew she started settling steadily into the water.

The bows of ships are one of the strongest sections of a vessel and are designed to withstand head-on collision. Although the *Renée Marthe* 's bows were badly damaged in the collision, she remained afloat and was taken into Dartmouth for repair.

The Torbay Boom Defence Vessel arrived on the scene and Captain Johannesson accepted a tow from it whilst most of his crew were taken off the *Bretagne* to safety. Captain Johannesson stayed aboard with his First Mate, Mr Harry Watterson, and a naval gunner, Mr Richard Pym. The three men desperately tried to uncouple the jammed steering gear as the *Bretagne*, with her rudder jammed to starboard, could not even be towed in a straight line. They were not however able to free the steering gear and it soon became clear that she was doomed.

The *Bretagne* continued to settle into the water steadily. Soon, waves were starting to wash the decks and at this stage Captain Johannesson ordered his two remaining men into a lifeboat. The First Mate, however, decided to go back down below decks to try to save his personal possessions and money. Sadly he had left it too late – a wave swept over the deck and slammed a door behind him, and he was trapped. He was unable to get back out of the ship before it sank and it took him with it into the depths. Captain Johannesson and the gunner could do nothing to help and were forced to step into the lifeboat just as the *Bretagne* disappeared beneath the waves forever.

Within one short hour of the collision occurring, the waters had closed over the *Bretagne* and she had sunk down to the bottom in a depth of 25 metres.

The Torbay Boom Defence Vessel returned with the remaining crew to Torquay. Despite the trauma of the loss of the vessel, Gunner Pym was not permitted to visit his parents' home in Torquay to let them know he was safe. He was ordered to report directly to Devonport, as his No. 1 uniform had gone down with the ship.

In the years following the sinking, the *Bretagne* became just one more of the innumerable shipwrecks that litter the English Channel. Her cargo of coal would be difficult to salvage at that time and the cost of recovering it would far outweigh its commercial value. It simply wasn't worth lifting the coal. There was nothing else on the *Bretagne* that merited the attentions of commercial salvers, and so the ship and her cargo were left to lie in the depths.

As the years passed, memories of her faded and her exact identity became forgotten to most people. As the Depression of the 1930s gave way to yet another global conflict, the Second World War, the English Channel would again find itself becoming host to further countless wrecks, a legacy of man's inhumanity to man.

In the post-war years the world-famous commercial salvage company Risden Beazley Ltd salvaged cargoes, propellers and engines from practically all the commercially viable shipwrecks around Britain's shores. The *Bretagne*'s cargo and fitments did not attract their attention or that of other salvers.

By the 1960s the identity of the wreck had been lost, although its position was known, and it was simply called the Teignmouth Coal Boat by local fishermen who had buoyed it. In 1966 the Bristol Aeroplane Company branch of the BSAC dived the wreck from a chartered hard boat and a heavily encrusted bell was located and recovered. When the 50 years of encrustation was removed from the bell, its legend was revealed:

Bretagne
1903
Christiania

The Teignmouth Coal Boat had at last given up its identity. Christiania was recognised as being the old name for Oslo, the Norwegian city where she had been built. Once her name and place of building were uncovered, research could be carried out into the circumstances of how she came to be lying at the bottom of the sea.

That research revealed that the vessel had been requisitioned in 1916 from her owners, Messrs Copper and Alexander, London, during the First World War by the Ministry for War Shipping. As a war loss, ownership of the vessel was now vested in the present-day Ministry of Transport. Negotiations were opened with the Ministry and the wreck was eventually purchased for the sum of £30 by an individual diver who in turn sold the wreck on to the Bristol Aeroplane branch of the British Sub-Aqua Club, now the British Aerospace Sub-Aqua Club who own the vessel to this day.

Portholes, china and navigation lanterns were subsequently recovered from the wreck along with a brass nameplate marked 'R. Pym, Devon'. During research the crew list had been traced and a Richard Pym was listed as one of two naval gunners responsible for manning the stern defensive 12-pounder gun. Further investigations led to Mr Pym being traced and found to be living with his daughter in Torquay.

In 1972 the Bristol branch of the BSAC used a necklace of plaster gelignite to successfully separate the 12-pounder stern gun from its mounting. The explosives were set in position by divers and 150 feet of detonating fuse cord was then run out from the charges to a surface vessel. Once the divers were back on the surface and all out of the water the detonator was attached to the surface end of the detonating fuse. The fuse was lit and then attached to a float and cast off. The surface vessel then cleared the area. Ninety seconds later the charge detonated and the sea frothed and boiled above the stern of the wreck. Once things settled down, divers were sent down and found that the plan had worked – the gun was now lying on the deck, detached from its mounting.

Some weeks later oil drums and canisters were attached to the gun and gradually filled with air to give lift. The gun, its weight countered by the buoyancy of the oil drums, was initially pulled in by hand, using ropes. As it lifted nearer the surface the expanding air in the drums took over and carried the gun upwards. The drums broke the surface and, after more than half a century in the depths, the gun saw the light of day once more. It was secured to the surface vessel, the 60-foot MFV *Bowmark* and towed back to Torquay. Once there, the gun was lifted by the harbour crane and lowered onto a trailer. In a fitting gesture the divers then took the gun to the home of the then 79-year-old Mr Richard Pym, the actual gunner on the vessel when it had gone down. After 54 years, gunner and gun were reunited.

Today the wreck of the once-graceful steamship *Bretagne* lies in a general depth ranging from 24 to a maximum of 30msw at the stern. She rests a few miles offshore from Teignmouth in Babbacombe Bay, and is widely regarded as one of East Devon's most popular wrecks.

The wreck rests on an even keel, her bows pointing to the south-west. She is

THE WRECK OF THE BEAUTIFUL SCHOONER-RIGGED SS *BRETAGNE.* © ROD MACDONALD 2003

largely structurally intact and retains her complete ship shape. The least depth to her decks is about 22–24msw and she therefore makes an interesting dive suitable for most levels of diver. She is best dived at slack water but, lying out of the main tidal streams, is diveable at most states of the tide.

The *Bretagne* sits proudly upright on her keel in the silent depths. The straight stem of her bows is now covered in a carpet of anemones and makes an impressive sight. The wreck, once home to man, has now become an underwater reef, home to a myriad of fish, crabs, lobsters and soft corals which all find both food and protection in her rotting skeleton. The hull is almost completely covered by soft corals, anemones, sea squirts and the gruesomely named 'Dead Men's Fingers'.

Up on the foredeck, the sturdy anchor winch sits squarely on the centre line of the vessel with robust anchor chains rising up from her chain lockers to the winch and on to the anchor hawse pipes. Both anchors, however, are no longer to be found in their hawses. Forward of the black and foreboding opening into the foredeck holds, Hatch No. 1, a raised companionway doorway leads below decks. There are two further deckhouses set one at either side of the hull here. The starboard-side deckhouse houses a small toilet whilst the port-side deckhouse was formerly the rigging store. The foredeck itself has two 15-feet rectangular hatches leading into the two holds below. The foremast originally stood between the two hatches but has long since fallen or been swept away.

Either side of the foremast's original location in between Hatches 1 and 2, cargo winches are set on the deck, fore and aft. These were used to operate the derrick system for loading and unloading the holds. The holds themselves are still full of the original cargo of Welsh steam coal but that cargo is now covered with a thick layer of silt which billows up at the downdraught from careless finning. The whole foredeck, hatch rims and all, is collapsing down onto the cargo of coal.

The decking itself at either side of the hatches has rotted away in places to reveal the structural beams of the ship's frame. Here and there these beams too have rotted and detached themselves from the starboard side of the hull. This has allowed the deck itself to collapse downwards to the shelter deck level below.

Aft of Hatch No. 2 stands the remnants of the *Bretagne*'s bridge superstructure. This originally rose up several deck levels above the main deck and had a covered walkway at either side to allow passage fore and aft. The *Bretagne* was wire-swept a long time ago by the Royal Navy to reduce any obstruction to shipping. This sweep was probably responsible for removing the foremast and also did a good job of removing most of the bridge superstructure, although part of it now hangs over the starboard side. Where the bridge was originally situated there are just a few spars and struts sticking up at awkward angles to mark its former location.

Aft of the remnants of the bridge superstructure stands the deckhouse which covered the boiler-room and engine-room down in the innards of the hull itself. The once-tall funnel rose up from this deckhouse but, made of thin, lightweight metal, has long since rotted away. Now, a cavernous, round, black hole in the roof of the deckhouse, with just a few inches of the rim of the funnel remaining, marks its former position and leads down to the boiler-room below.

On the main deck either side of this deckhouse are small rectangular openings, the coal chutes for loading coal down into her bunkers. Doors on either side of this deckhouse allow access into the cavernous spaces of the engine-room itself. The small pitched roof of the engine-room with its skylights, the glass long gone, is an easy guide to the engine-room location. A large slit opening, running the breadth of the deckhouse athwartships, and aft of the funnel, would have allowed heavy engine machinery to be manoeuvred down into the hull. Entering the engine-room, the triple expansion engine itself sits on the centre line of the vessel and it is one of the highlights of diving the *Bretagne* to follow the workings of her engine-room. Covered walkways ran down either side of this deckhouse, the structural spars still visible leading from the gunwales up to the top of the superstructure.

Although the *Bretagne* had two foredeck holds, she was only fitted out with one on her aftmost section. The hatch cover is long gone leaving a couple of support beams running across the hatch opening. The hatch allows easy access down into the cavernous hold. Forward of the hatch, and between it and the engine-room deckhouse, stands the stump of the main mast. The mast itself, like the foremast, is long gone, probably broken off in a wire sweep. Two sturdy cargo winches are set on the deck aft of the main mast stump and would have worked a derrick system for loading and unloading the hold.

On the starboard side of the hull at this hold, the hull of the *Bretagne* has been cut open vertically as though with a large knife. This is the telling evidence of the ferocity and power of the fateful blow from the bows of the *Renée Marthe* as she appeared suddenly out of the fog on that day of destiny in 1918. So wide is this gouge that divers can enter the hold through it and see the cargo of coal still stored there. Aft of this hatch, as is the custom with vessels of this era, a spare four-bladed propeller still sits securely chained to the deck, as if still ready to be deployed in the event of damage to the main propeller.

At the very stern itself, the deckhouse that served as a gun platform for the 12-pounder defensive gun still stands in situ. The remains of the wracking system for turning the gun are still evident although the gun itself was recovered from the wreck in 1972. Mooring bollards and cleats dot the sides of the hull and the decking here has rotted away, revealing the structural beams and framing of the ship. The rounded schooner stern is quite a magnificent sight and sheers away under the hull sharply. The rudder still stands in position part buried in the seabed and heeled slightly over to port. The propeller itself is still in place and visible, although a couple of its blades have been damaged. It is here at the stern that the greatest depth on a dive on *Bretagne* of 30msw can be found.

The *Bretagne* is a magnificent dive. At just 236 feet in length she is small enough that she can be fairly comprehensively explored in a single dive. She is a neat compact steamship and more than 80 years after her sinking you can still tell that she was a well-run ship, with everything neatly squared away in the right place. The depth she sits in is such that divers can get a long time down on her in any one dive, particularly if Nitrox is being used.

The *Bretagne* has become a marine ecosystem – there is all the sealife to admire as well as the wreck itself. Schools of fish drift over her, congregating around the imposing and majestic schooner stern. Her wreck will hold something of interest for all divers, from beginners to the more experienced wanting to explore her holds and engine-rooms. The *Bretagne* is a wreck that will find its way into most divers' logbooks at some stage.

Essential Information

BOAT LAUNCH SITE: The slip next to the Teign Diving Centre is useable at all states of the tide except low springs. There are other slips at most ports along the East Devon coastline.

HARD BOAT DIVING: Divers Down, 139 Babbacombe Road, Babbacombe, Torquay (01803) 327111 run regular trips out from the small breakwater at Babbacombe Beach. They use two Offshore 105s, *Atlantis* and *Grace II*, and have an 8.5m RIB. The road down to the breakwater is very steep and angled, not for the faint-hearted.

Teign Diving Centre also cover the *Bretagne* as one of their regular dive sites (01626) 772965. Many other charter boats work from Exmouth, Torquay, Paignton and Brixham.

TIDAL CONDITIONS: Whilst slack water is always preferable for diving, the *Bretagne*

DIVE DETAILS FOR THE SS *BRETAGNE*

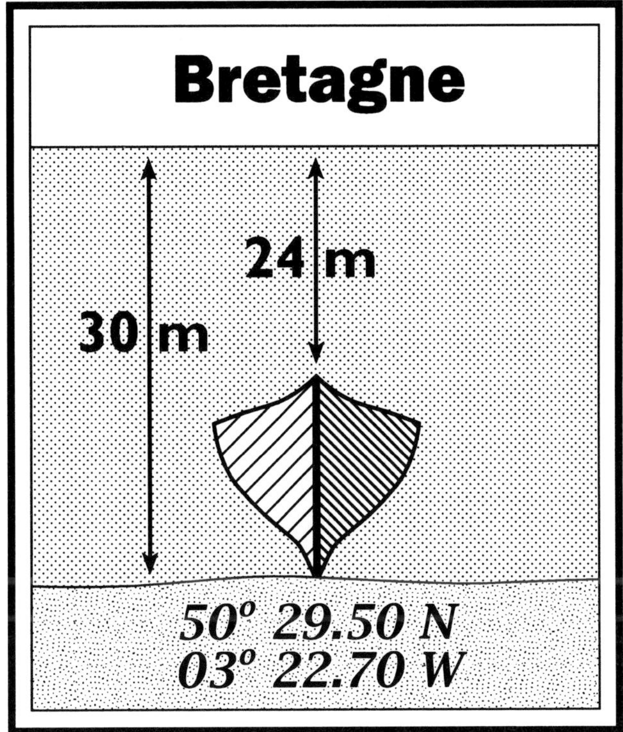

sits in an area that is not badly affected by tide and so she can be dived at most states of the tide.

VISIBILITY: In the settled summer months, 5-metre visibility is an average, however, the wreck does sit in an area of poor visibility and often the visibility can be less, at 2–3 metres.

MAXIMUM DEPTH: 30msw on the seabed at the stern.

LEAST DEPTH: 22msw to deck.

COASTGUARD: Brixham Coastguard (01803) 882704.

RECOMPRESSION CHAMBERS FACILITIES: Fort Bovisand, Plymouth.

AIR SUPPLIES: Divers Down, Babbacombe has air, Nitrox and Trimix to 300 Bar (01803) 327111. Teign Diving Centre provide air and Nitrox fills (01626) 772965.

HYDROGRAPHIC CHART: Berry Head to Bill of Portland, No. 3315.

POSITION: Lat 50 29.50 N, Long 03 22.70 W.

DIVER LEVEL: The relatively shallow depth and lack of tide affecting this wreck make it suitable for most levels of diver from BSAC Sports Diver and above.

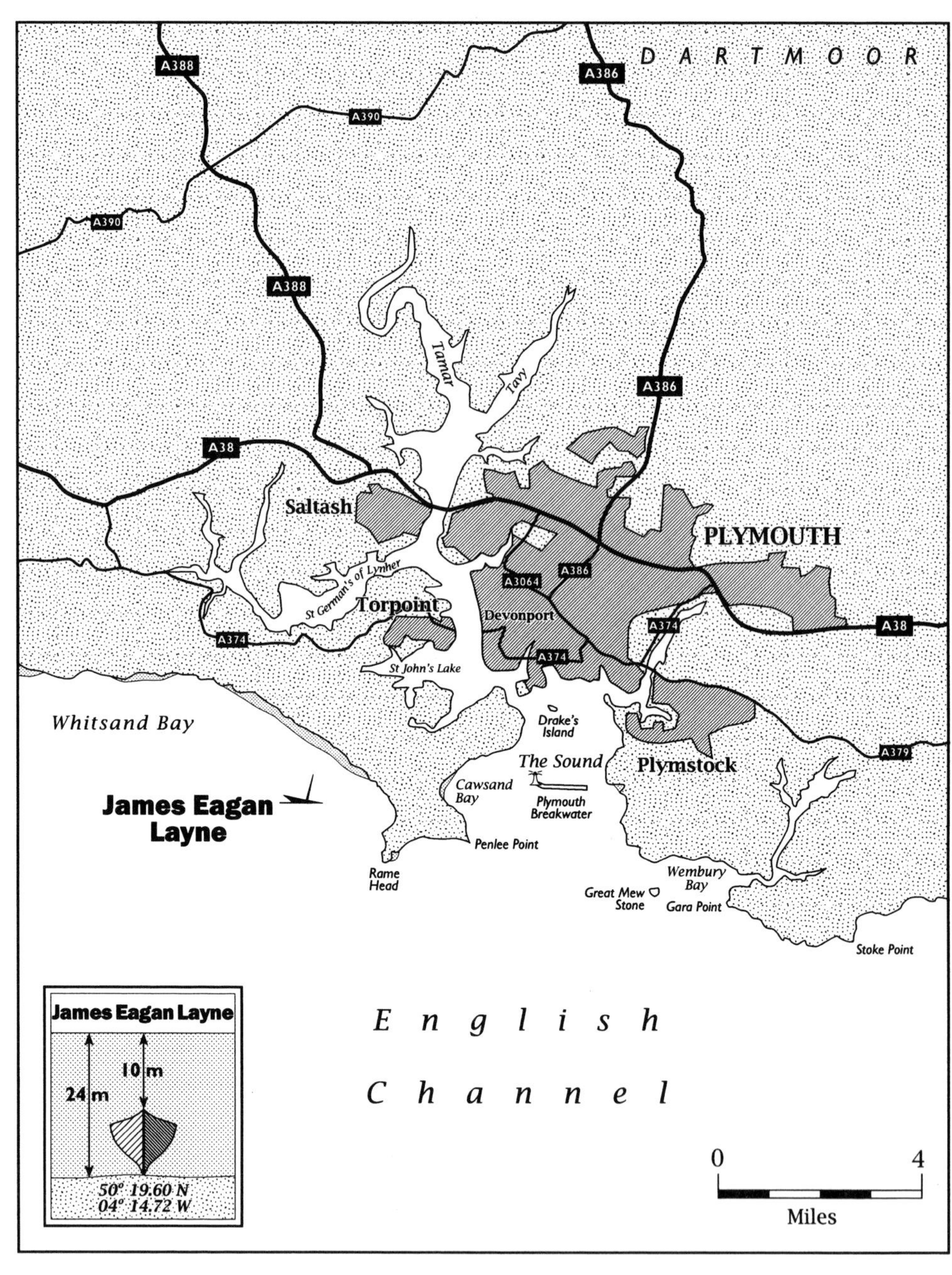
DARTMOOR
A388
A386
A390
A390
A388
Tamar
Tavy
A386
A38
Saltash
PLYMOUTH
St German's of Lynher
A3064
A386
Torpoint
Devonport
A374
A374
A38
A374
St John's Lake
Whitsand Bay
Drake's Island
The Sound
Plymstock
A379
Cawsand Bay
Plymouth Breakwater
James Eagan Layne
Penlee Point
Rame Head
Wembury Bay
Great Mew Stone
Gara Point
Stoke Point
James Eagan Layne
10 m
24 m
50° 19.60 N
04° 14.72 W
English Channel
0
4
Miles

OPPOSITE PAGE: LOCATION CHART FOR THE AMERICAN LIBERTY SHIP *JAMES EAGAN LAYNE*, WHITSAND BAY, CORNWALL

CHAPTER 7

JAMES EAGAN LAYNE, WHITSAND BAY, CORNWALL

The wreck of the American Liberty ship *James Eagan Layne* is perhaps one of the most famous in British diving. She sits on her keel in relatively shallow water of 24msw in Whitsand Bay, Cornwall, about three quarters of a mile offshore with a least depth down to her decks of just 10msw. She is usually buoyed at the very tip of her raised bow, only some 5 metres beneath the surface.

The *James Eagan Layne*, although well rotted, retains her ship shape from the bow right back to her engine-room and

PROFILE OF AN AMERICAN LIBERTY SHIP *SAMINVER*. PHOTO COURTESY OF THE IMPERIAL WAR MUSEUM, LONDON

the aft holds. Three large open cargo hatches allow divers to drift down into the cavernous holds beneath her foredeck. The main deck itself is rotted, with only the transverse beams of her frame remaining in places. The bulkheads that once would have separated the holds below the main deck are now gone and it is possible to pass from one hold to the next below deck without having to rise up onto the main deck.

The engine-room area has been salvaged and opened up, making the large engine block itself, sitting on the centre line of the vessel, easily accessible. Aft of the engine-room the wreck loses its shape, but there is still a lot to see as her innards and cargo lie scattered about. A large detached section of her stern marks the end of the wreckage.

The *James Eagan Layne* is a classic wreck dive on one of a class of vessels, the Liberty ships, which were produced as standard ships in huge numbers and at great speed to combat the loss of Allied shipping to U-boat activity in the Second World War. Quite simply, ships like her won the Battle of the Atlantic. Without them the Allies would not have been able to ship sufficient quantities of war supplies to Great Britain. There would have been no D-day and perhaps no Allied victory. Their role in the Second World War was absolutely vital.

This famous wreck dive is suitable for all levels of scuba diver, from the novice making a first wreck dive, to the more experienced wreck diver who, because of the shallow depth and long dive times possible, can do some serious wreck exploration.

The *James Eagan Layne* was built in 1944 at the Delta Shipbuilding Company's yard in New Orleans for the United States War Shipping Administration. The Liberty shipbuilding programme had been started in 1940, at a time when America had not yet entered the war and Britain stood alone against the might of the German war machine. German U-boats were sinking British shipping faster than replacement ships could be turned out by the British yards. It was the 'happy time' for U-boats. In the first nine months of the war, 150 British ships were sent to the bottom, most being victims of U-boat attack.

The British government realised that the war effort depended on imports of materials and vital products like oil. Without sufficient internal natural resources, Britain had to import by sea. With the high rate of shipping losses Britain was slowly bleeding to death and would soon be powerless to defend itself against the Nazi threat. In September 1940, just a year into the war, Britain turned to America for help. Franklin D. Roosevelt agreed to the request announcing to Congress: 'Our most useful and immediate role is to act as an arsenal for them

[Britain] as well as for ourselves. We shall send in ever-increasing numbers, ships, planes, tanks and guns. That is our purpose and our pledge.'

America agreed initially to build 60 ships. Although they were to follow an antiquated design, this type of vessel was quick and easy to build and, importantly, reliable. The American government also then decided to replace its reserve of numerous but obsolete merchant vessels, many of which had been stacked in inland rivers and waterways since the end of the First World War, with a modified version of the British design. The Americans formulated an idea of the engine required and a model of the proposed class of ship was made up. When it was presented to President Roosevelt, he famously commented that it was an 'ugly duckling', but that it would get the job done. The tag of 'Ugly Duckling' stuck and it was to try and improve the image of the ships that they were christened the Liberty Fleet. History had just been made.

Initially, a 200-ship bulk-building programme got underway to mass-produce ships for Britain. The ships were constructed to a standard design, much like the standard ships of the First World War. The aim was to try and build these ships in much the same way as a car assembly line. As many sub-assemblies as possible were prefabricated, such as superstructures and hull sections, and attempts were made to eliminate all unnecessary tasks. The ships were all welded, as opposed to being drilled and riveted and full-size wooden templates were used for cutting out sections of steel. All had standard oil-fired engines which produced a standard maximum speed of 11 knots and all had a standard tonnage of 7,176 gross.

The first of the Liberty ships, the *Patrick Henry*, was launched in September 1941. On 27 September 1941, 14 new ships were launched and it was christened Liberty Day. Just two months later America joined the war. The Battle of the Atlantic changed from being Britain's sole fight – it became America's fight too. Roosevelt declared that to beat the U-boat menace America would build a Bridge of Ships over the Atlantic. The aim was to mass-produce ships faster than they could be sunk. It would be a war of attrition.

New shipyards were opened up and down America's coasts, and a huge number of new shipyard workers were recruited from across the country, from farms and all walks of life. About one quarter of the new workers had never even seen the sea before arriving at their new place of employment at a shipyard on the coast, but these were not unskilled labourers. Many were men and women from farms across America, used to working with their hands, with mechanical and engineering skills. The new shipyards each employed about 15,000 people. The yards were a mass of steel sections and plates and they echoed to a cacophony of sound, from drilling, riveting and working steel. Explosions of sparks flew around from welding and cutting works and large sections of ship were craned around into position. The shipyard workers commonly worked very long shifts of 16–18 hours but the prevailing view was that this was the ordinary man and woman's way of helping the fight. It became a passionate and driving way of life. About one-third of the workforce were women.

The first Liberty ships took 150 days to build and about 95 to kit out. Each ship was constructed from 250,000 individual parts and had about 43 miles of welding, 5 miles of wire and 7 miles of pipework. The ships were considered expendable and a single successful transatlantic crossing justified the construction costs of up to $2m per ship. They were only made for the one trip. Anything more was a bonus.

The USA was now also at war in the Pacific, and so more ships were needed for that theatre, to transport men and the machines and parts of war. The Americans went on to develop and improve their production systems and the build rate improved dramatically. By 1942 the fastest build had been cut to just 47 days. In 1942 and 1943 some 1,500 Liberty ships were mass-produced and in 1944 some 800 more were produced, of which the *James Eagan Layne* was but one. The record for completion of a single ship tumbled from 47 days to 15 days, then 10 days, and soon to just 7 days from laying down her keel to completion. That same year the fastest Liberty ship build was completed with the *Robert E. Peary* being launched in an amazing 4 days and 15 hours after her keel was laid. Three days later it was on its way serving its vital role. These record feats were more publicity or propaganda stunts and the common time for producing and completing a Liberty ship was about 50 days.

The huge American shipbuilding programme saved Britain in the Battle of the Atlantic. In all, some 2,700 Liberty ships were produced. At the same time the volume of materials reaching Britain increased. The 'Ugly Ducklings' were designed to be able to carry anything and they transported a huge mass of war materials, planes, tanks, railway wagons and supplies across the Atlantic for the Allied war effort.

Each Atlantic crossing was filled with danger for the crews of the Liberty ships. They were told that as soon as they left port in America they were in hostile territory. The ships were armed for protection with a Naval gun crew of 36 in addition to the crew.

The ships would cross the Atlantic in convoys, typically of about 60 ships in a box formation on a broad front. Outside the box, anti-submarine warships would patrol, anxiously trying to keep their charges safe. The top speed of the Liberty ships was just 11 knots and the convoys were slow, typically moving at about 7 knots. The two outer lines of ships in the box were the most vulnerable and so fuel tankers and ammunition ships were centred near the middle for added protection. The worst place to be came to be known as 'Coffin Corner'.

THE GUNS OF A BRITISH DESTROYER PROTECT AN AMERICAN LIBERTY SHIP IN DANGEROUS WATERS.
PHOTO COURTESY OF IMPERIAL WAR MUSEUM, LONDON

This was the last ship at the back at either side, the easiest target for a U-boat to pick off. If a ship broke down, the convoy would not stop but left it behind without escort, again easy prey for a U-boat. If the problem could be fixed the straggler would dash to make up ground and rejoin the convoy.

The *James Eagan Layne* herself was the first ship to be named after an American merchant seaman, an engineer who had died in action in April 1942 when his ship, the *Esso Baton Rouge*, was torpedoed off the east coast of the United States. In a fitting tribute the late James Eagan Layne's widow was invited to launch the vessel.

The *James Eagan Layne* was 422.8 feet in length with a beam of 57 feet and draught of 34.8 feet. She had two decks, the standard cruiser stern and oil-fuelled triple-expansion engine. Her gross tonnage was 7,176, her net tonnage 4,380. Her keel was laid on 23 October 1944 and just 40 days later she was launched sideways into the Mississippi on 2 December 1944. It took just 16 days to kit her out and she was then ready for delivery – an impressive and speedy piece of shipbuilding. After delivery the *James Eagan Layne* crossed the Atlantic to Britain. Her career at sea, however, was to be cut short after only three months' war service. On 21 March 1945 she would be torpedoed and sunk by *U-1195*.

After safely crossing the dangerous waters of the Atlantic to Britain, the *James Eagan Layne* found herself at the southern Welsh port of Barry, which opens onto the north side of the Bristol Channel. Once docked, her cavernous holds were filled with a general war cargo that included tank parts, jeeps, lorries and railway rolling stock along with general US Army engineering stores, motorboats and timber.

Once lading was completed, her mooring lines were cast off and she set out on a voyage to Ghent in Belgium. Her precious cargo was intended for General Patton's Third Army, whose tanks were racing forward in a bid to reach the Rhine at Ludwigshafen. *James Eagan Layne*'s tank spares were for those Sherman tanks. She was manned by a crew of 42 and also carried 27 armed guards, marines whose job included manning defensive anti-aircraft guns.

After leaving Barry, the *James Eagan Layne* headed out along the Bristol Channel to sea before turning southwards and running down the northern shores of Devon and Cornwall. Turning at Land's End, the most southerly point of the mainland, she entered the English Channel and headed eastwards. Lizard Point and Falmouth passed by on her port beam. She was soon approaching Plymouth, but was unknowingly moving into the sights of a hidden killer, the Type VIIC U-boat, *U-1195*.

U-1195 had been laid down at Schichau, Danzig, on 6 February 1943 and commissioned on 4 November 1943. The Type VIIC class of U-boat was the workhorse of the German U-boat force during the Second World War, being a slightly modified version of the successful VIIB. The Type VIICs had basically the same engine layout and power, but were slightly larger and heavier so making them slightly slower than the Type VIIBs. At 67.1 metres long with a beam of 6.2 metres the Type VIICs displaced 769 tons on the surface and 871 submerged. They carried 14 torpedoes, most being fitted out with 5 torpedo tubes, 4 at the bow and 1 at the stern. The VIIC carried 26 mines and had a surface speed of 17.7 knots and 7.6 knots submerged. The first Type VIIC, *U-69*, was commissioned in 1940 with the remainder of her class coming into service as the 'happy days' were almost over. It was the Type VIIC that faced the final defeat to the Allied anti-submarine campaign in late 1943 and 1944.

After her commission on 4 November 1943, *U-1195* initially served as a school boat and then latterly until 31 December 1944 she served as a training boat. Then, on 1 January 1945, she went out on her first patrol. Although she would sink the *James Eagan Layne* on this first patrol, it would also be her last.

Under the command of Kapitänleutnant Ernst Cordes, *U-1195* detected *James Eagan Layne* and Cordes manoeuvred his boat for a shot at her. Once in position he fired unseen. The torpedo ran straight and true and struck the unsuspecting *James Eagan Layne* near her engine-room. The position of the strike was noted on *James Eagan Layne* as 50 13 30 N, 04 14 W.

James Eagan Layne was mortally wounded by this torpedo strike, but she did not sink immediately. Water flooding into her hull soon put her engines out of action and the vessel slewed to a wallowing halt. A coded 'sub-attack' message was immediately sent off. The crew of 42 and the 27 armed guards aboard knew that their attacker may well still be lying submerged close by studying its prey, watching through a periscope to see if the single torpedo blow was a fatal one which would send the prey to the bottom – or whether another precious torpedo would be required to finish the job.

The crew on the *James Eagan Layne* were at action stations. Look-outs were tensed, peering out to seaward, straining their eyes for the tell-tale track of another torpedo sent by a cruel and uncaring foe to complete the destruction of their vessel and send it to the bottom before it could be saved.

Soon, however, Navy frigates out of nearby Plymouth arrived on the scene and set about depth-charging U-1195's suspected position. As this was being done two Admiralty tugs, HMS *Flaunt* and HMS *Atlas*, arrived and attached towing hawsers. A deadly race against time had been started – would they have time to tow the *James Eagan Layne* to safety and save her valuable and vital war cargo, or would she succumb to the inrushing water? Her aft holds had been badly damaged and the water level was rising fast.

At first the tugs headed for Plymouth but the *James Eagan Layne* continued to settle deeper into the water. It soon became clear that she would not remain afloat long enough to reach the safety of the port. The decision was then taken to redirect the tow and head for Whitsand Bay, where it was hoped she could be run aground on the soft sandy seabed there. If that were successful, both the ship and her precious cargo would be saved.

Unfortunately, the rate of water filling her hull was simply too fast – time ran out for the *James Eagan Layne* and she sank not far offshore in 22msw of water, her bow just 5msw beneath the waves.

U-1195 escaped the depth-charging by Navy frigates and was able to leave the scene unscathed to continue on her first patrol. During the following two weeks at sea she sank one other Allied vessel. However, 16 days later on 7 April 1945 her luck would run out. Some distance to the south of the Isle of Wight in the English Channel at a reported position of 50.33.17 N, 00.56.09 W she was sunk by depth charges from the British destroyer HMS *Watchman*. Although all the crew of 42 and the 27 armed guards aboard the *James Eagan Layne* had survived the attack by *U-1195*, 32 of the crew of *U-1195* perished in the attack by *HMS Watchman*. There were 18 survivors. In her short career, *U-1195* had sunk two Allied vessels, a total of 18,614 tons.

The *James Eagan Layne*'s valuable tank spares, lying in her wreck in such shallow water close to Plymouth's naval facilities, were easy to salvage for re-use during the war. Salvage thereafter ground to a halt and the wreck of the *James Eagan Layne* was left to lie on the seabed in peace. Her foremast rose up from the main deck and jutted out of the water marking her position.

In 1953 the US government sold her hull as scrap to an Icelandic firm. That firm however did not complete the contract and once again, for a short few years she was left to lie undisturbed in the silence of the sea.

In the 1960s, her prop was blown off and salvaged and in increasing numbers sport divers started visiting her remains. In 1976, however, a complete ban on diving her was enforced following the discovery of radioactive discs in her cargo. Navy divers were guided by BSAC divers to the location of the discs, which were in lead-covered cases containing 240 discs each. Some had spilled loose. Around 2,000 discs in all were collected before the wreck was declared safe for diving again.

Today the wreck of the Liberty ship *James Eagan Layne* in Whitsand Bay is normally buoyed with a line fixed to the strongest part of her, the raised section of her bow, which comes to just 5 metres beneath the surface. The seabed itself is at a depth of about 20msw.

The ship steps down from the very tip of the raised bow to the main deck at about 8–10msw. With a beam of 57 feet she is almost 20 metres wide so there is a lot to see on this expanse of decking. The actual plating itself has mostly rotted away leaving a latticework of cross-sectional beams and framing.

Here on the foredeck can be found three large rectangular cargo hatches some 20 feet wide. The wooden hatch-covers have long ago been turned to silt by the sea and the open hatches allow free and unhindered access below deck into the business end of the Liberty ship, its huge cargo holds. With lots of light penetrating down into the holds themselves through the rotted deck-plating and open hatches, divers can easily drift down through the hatches to explore the innards of the holds. The bulkheads that would have separated the holds are also long rotted away to form one large common space. It is now possible to pass from one hold to the next below the main deck.

Aft of Hatch No. 3 lies the area where the superstructure and funnel would have been. There is now no trace of the superstructure – it is as though the whole deckhouse has been blown and lifted clear of the wreck, opening up the engine-room to the sky. On the port side, on the remnants of the main deck can be found a small deckhouse, most probably a latrine.

THE REMAINS OF THE AMERICAN LIBERTY SHIP *JAMES EAGAN LAYNE* IN WHITSAND BAY, CORNWALL. COPYRIGHT ROD MACDONALD 2003

In the engine-room area the most striking feature is the massive oil-fuelled triple-expansion engine, the very heart of the ship itself, which sits fore and aft on the centre line of the vessel. The diameter of the cylinders was 24.5 inches, 37 inches and 70 inches and the stroke was 48 inches. Aft of the engine are the remains of the boiler-room with her large boilers still open for inspection by divers. Passing aft from the boiler-room area, divers now reach the section of ship that would have been aft of the central superstructure. This is where the ship broke and the whole ship is collapsed with large sections of the ship's side-plating lying flat on the seabed which is littered with spilled cargo. In the debris the prop tunnel runs aft, leading the divers towards the stern section.

In this area, the ship loses its shape completely and of the original structure of Hatches 4 and 5 there is no trace. But the area is still interesting, as the cargo from these holds is strewn about on the seabed and allows a glimpse of the role the *James Eagan Layne* was playing at the time of her demise. Hundreds of Viking-Johnson (or V-J) couplings lie on the seabed in piles. These couplings, still in use today, were made by the Victaulic Company in America and could join two unequal pipes together with flanges and an 8-inch rubber ring.

The actual stern section of the ship has broken off the main

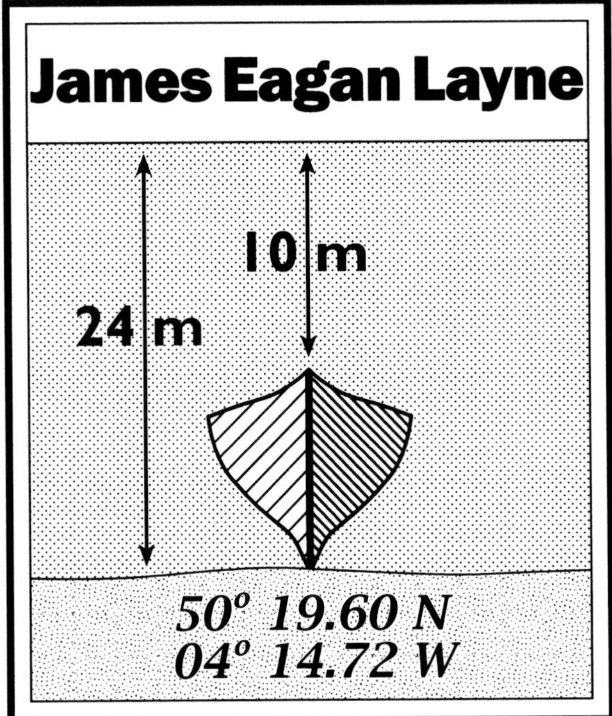

DIVE DETAILS FOR THE AMERICAN LIBERTY SHIP *JAMES EAGAN LAYNE*

wreck and lies detached some 50m away. This 50-foot-long section lies on its starboard side at an angle of 45 degrees. The rudder is still attached, along with the steering quadrant complete with its chains and winches.

The wreck of the *James Eagan Layne* has become an artificial reef providing food and refuge for myriad forms of sealife. Large collections of Plumrose anemones and the soft coral named 'Dead Men's Fingers' festoon the steel structure of the wreck itself. Cod, pollack and Black Bass drift over and through the skeleton of the wreck. Conger eels and lobsters hide in the nooks and crannies whilst massive edible crabs rummage for food in the debris.

The wreck of the *James Eagan Layne* makes a fascinating dive and one that is regularly visited by divers. Her remains are a classic wreck dive with an intriguing historical perspective, lots of atmospheric spaces to investigate and well populated by sealife. It is a wreck that most UK wreck divers will have in their logbooks, many, many times.

Essential Information

BOAT LAUNCH SITE: A number of hard boats run shuttles from Plymouth out to the wreck. Inflatables can be launched at numerous slips in Plymouth and at Fort Bovisand.
TIDAL CONDITIONS: Diveable at all states of tide.
VISIBILITY: 5–10 metres.
MAXIMUM DEPTH: 20msw.
LEAST DEPTH: 5msw. Main deck, 10msw.
COASTGUARD: Brixham Coastguard (01803) 882704.
RECOMPRESSION FACILITIES: DDRC (Diving Diseases Research Centre) Plymouth (01752) 209999.
AIR SUPPLIES: Deep Blue Diving, The Mountbatten Centre, Plymouth (01752) 491490. Nitrox, Air to 320 Bar, Trimix and premix EAN32.
HYDROGRAPHIC CHART: Plymouth to Salcombe, No. 5602.4.
POSITION: Lat 50 19.602 N, Long 004 14.715 W.
DIVER LEVEL: Suitable for all levels of diver.

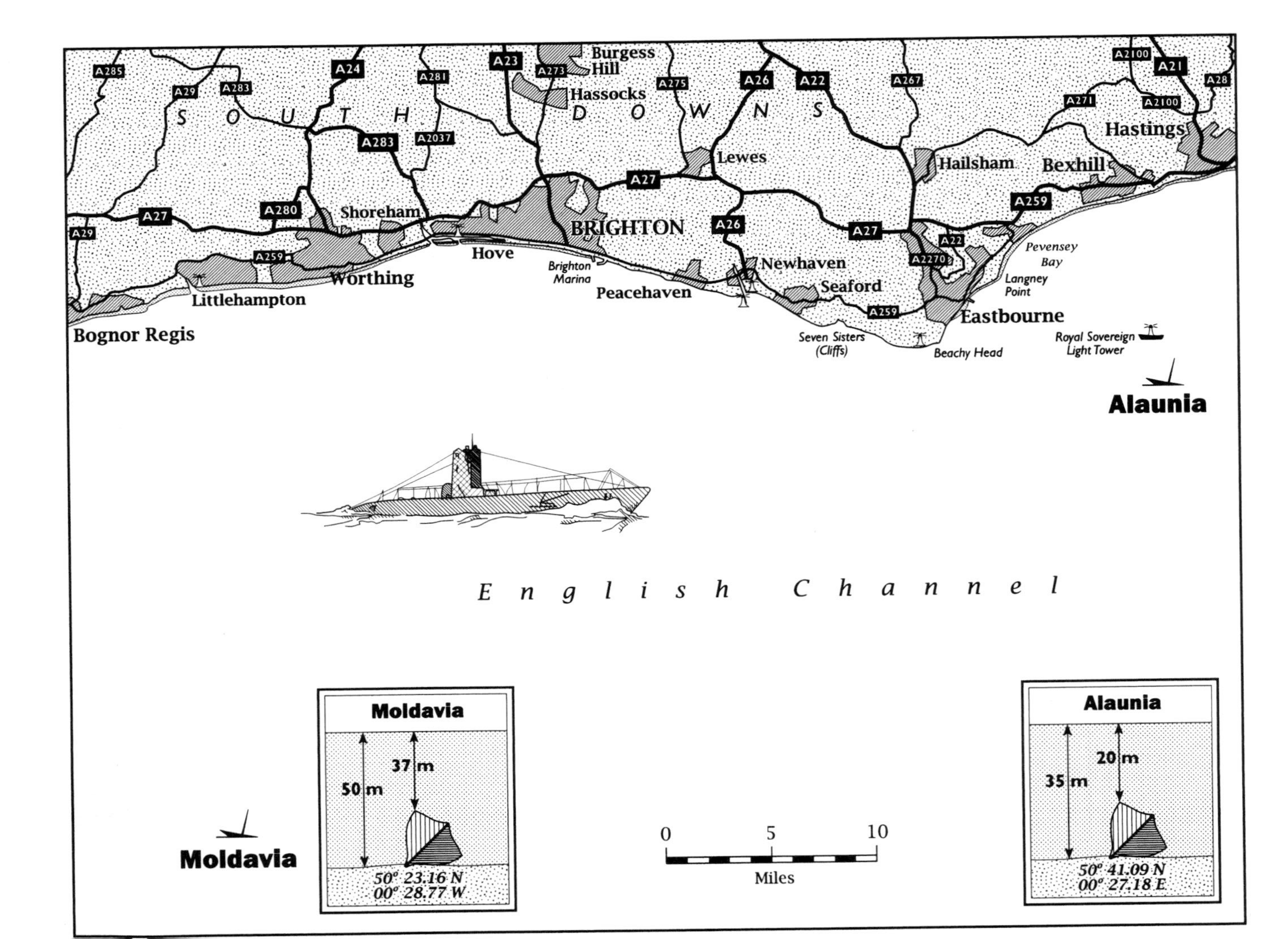

S O U T H D O W N S
Burgess Hill
Hassocks
Lewes
Hailsham
Hastings
Bexhill
Shoreham
BRIGHTON
Hove
Worthing
Littlehampton
Bognor Regis
Brighton Marina
Peacehaven
Newhaven
Seaford
Eastbourne
Pevensey Bay
Langney Point
Seven Sisters (Cliffs)
Beachy Head
Royal Sovereign Light Tower
A285
A29
A283
A24
A281
A23
A273
A275
A26
A22
A267
A2100
A21
A28
A271
A283
A2037
A280
A27
A259
A2270
Alaunia
English Channel
Moldavia
37 m
50 m
50° 23.16 N
00° 28.77 W
Alaunia
20 m
35 m
50° 41.09 N
00° 27.18 E
0
5
10
Miles

OPPOSITE: LOCATION CHART FOR WRECKS OF *MOLDAVIA* AND SS *ALAUNIA*

Chapter 8

THE *MOLDAVIA*, LITTLEHAMPTON, WEST SUSSEX

The British liner *Moldavia* is perhaps one of the most revered and well-loved wrecks in the English Channel. She lies a long way out in the Channel, some 26 miles, and so diving her becomes something of an expedition where everything must work in your favour. She is a deep dive too, some 50 metres or just over to the seabed, so your dive ability must be at the highest level for sport diving. Your dive kit must be well serviced and maintained. This far out in the Channel, if anything goes wrong at such a depth you are a long time away from emergency medical assistance.

THE MAJESTIC P&O LINER *MOLDAVIA*. PHOTO COURTESY OF NATIONAL MARITIME MUSEUM, GREENWICH

Twenty-six miles out to the site is a long way out by anybody's standards and it means a long boat journey of up to two hours each way. This is an exposed part of the Channel, very susceptible to unkind winds, so the seas must be calm and the weather in your favour. Twenty-six miles out is a long, long, uncomfortable journey in a pitching boat for those who have not yet acquired good sea legs. There is nothing worse than succumbing to sea-sickness on such a lengthy journey. There simply is no escape other than the old trick of staring grimly at the horizon. As the old saying goes, once sea-sickness starts to set in, 'First you think you are going to die, then you want to die.'

If the weather is kind, the winds light and the seas slight, you will be rewarded with a fabulous dive in renowned mid-Channel good visibility of 10–20 metres. The wreck itself is vast, hauntingly beautiful and still full of items of interest. Portholes hang open, their brass and glass fitments still in place. The massive anchors are still held snugly in their hawse pipes despite the ravages of more than 80 years at the bottom of the Channel. The sealife is immense. Large schools of fish drift over the wreck, sometimes hanging like a curtain obscuring large parts of it. The *Moldavia* is a must for every true wreck diver.

The *Moldavia* was a beautiful and massive passenger and mail ship built just after the turn of the last century for the Peninsular and Oriental Steam Navigation Company, the world-famous P&O. She was commissioned by the British Admiralty in 1915 and converted into an armed merchant cruiser during the dark days of the First World War. Bought outright by the Admiralty in 1916, she was soon afterwards turned over for use as a troopship. Two years later she would be sent to the bottom of the English Channel by *UB-57* – the same U-boat that would go on to sink the SS *Kyarra* (Chapter Four) the following day. Nearly 85 years later she still lies on the seabed and ranks as one of England's finest wreck dives.

The *Moldavia* was built in 1903 by J. Caird and Co., Greenock. She and her sister ship the *Mongolia* were the first of the 'M' type passenger and mail liners. She was 520 feet 6 inches in length with a beam of 58 feet 3 inches. She had a gross tonnage of 9,500 and net tonnage of 4,930.

The *Moldavia* was powered by two triple-expansion engines that developed 2,750 horsepower and drove her twin overlapping propellers to push her to speeds of 18.5 knots. To push such a huge mass through the water at such speeds the *Moldavia*'s steel propellers had to be a substantial 18 feet in diameter and were also fabricated by the builders, J. Caird and Co. Her international code signal was V.D.M.H.

The *Moldavia* was steel-built with three decks and six holds, the depth of hold being 33 feet 3 inches. She was fitted out with ten hydraulic cranes to work her cargoes and boasted a total cargo area of 90,000 cubic feet with 19,000 cubic feet. refrigerated space. Her two large raked-back funnels were set at the same angle as her stylish fore and main masts. The main central superstructure housed the bridge, captain's accommodation and saloons at the front, and extended back for almost half the length of the vessel rising up for two deck levels. Wooden lifeboats hung on davits either side atop it. At the very stern, another substantial superstructure gave further accommodation with yet more lifeboats hung above. In addition to a substantial cargo-carrying ability, the *Moldavia* could also carry 348 first-class passengers and 166 second-class. She was serviced by a crew of 370 and cost the princely sum of £336,178 to build.

After her launch, the *Moldavia* proceeded to London where she made her first scheduled sailing on 11 December 1903 from there, via Colombo and Melbourne, to Sydney. The *Moldavia* proved to be a beautiful liner which because of her design work was able to handle the seas she faced impeccably. She became a very famous ship, well known on the Britain to Australia run, and was a popular ship in the

THE P&O LINER *MOLDAVIA* ARRIVING AT FREMANTLE, WESTERN AUSTRALIA. MOORING ROPES HAVE BEEN LOOPED OVER BOLLARDS AND A WATCHFUL TUG SHEPHERDS HER AT THE STERN. THE CAPTAIN CAN BE SEEN AT THE PORTSIDE DOCKING BRIDGE SUPERVISING THE MANOEUVRE. PHOTO COURTESY OF THE BATTYE LIBRARY 9914P

years before the First World War. She ran aground on the Goodwins in 1907 but was floated off without incident.

After ten years of gracing the seas the carnage of the First World War erupted across Europe. Two years into the War, in 1915, the British government requisitioned the *Moldavia* for war service. She was fitted out with 4.7-inch guns and became the armed merchant cruiser, HMS *Moldavia*. Her armament was altered latterly with the substitution of her original guns by eight 6-inch guns. She had become a fast and powerfully armed cruiser.

In 1916 the British government bought her outright but in the period of time following the Battle of Jutland in 1916, when the German Navy was deterred from any further Fleet action against the Royal Navy, auxiliary cruisers such as *Moldavia* were no longer required and she was turned over for use as a troopship. It was in this role that the *Moldavia* would find herself on the American side of the Atlantic in 1918 being loaded with troops and supplies for what would be her final voyage.

It was the preceding April of 1917 that saw the United States declare war with Germany. Some seven months later, on 19 November 1917, as the full might of the huge American war effort gained momentum, the US War Department had directed that the organisation of the 4th Division of the Regular Army (RA) take place at Camp Greene in accordance with the Tables of Organisation of 8 August 1917. Between 3 December 1917 and 5 January 1918, that organisation was finalised and Major General George H. Cameron assumed command. The Division was made up of some 13,000 regular troops and was subdivided into infantry and artillery brigades. One of the brigades was the 8th Infantry Brigade, which included the 58th Infantry Regiment.

On 5 January 1918, organisation of the 4th Division (RA) was completed and the entire division began extensive training. On 21 April the Division had completed all its phases of training and was cleared for overseas movement to the battlefields of France. On 23 April the Division moved to Camp Mills New York, a staging for overseas movements by increments to Britain. The 39th Infantry Regiment sailed on the SS *Megantic* and arrived in the French port of Brest on 23 May. On 11 May, the 58th Regiment of the 8th Infantry Brigade, some 907 men, boarded the dazzle-painted *Moldavia* and ventured out for the long journey across the Atlantic to the killing fields of Europe.

The slow crossing of the Atlantic was completed successfully and on the night of 23 May 1918 the convoy, now consisting of five large steamships and their attendant naval protective destroyers, started up the English Channel, heading for France. Every single porthole was blacked out and no light at all that might give away the convoy was permitted on any of the ships. All aboard knew they were now entering the most dangerous part of their voyage, the U-boats' killing grounds.

Unbeknown to the convoy, Oberleutnant Johannes Lohs, in command of *UB-57* of the Flanders Flotilla, had left Zeebruge the evening before, 22 May, and successfully managed to take *UB-57* over the top of the Belgian coastal barrage, a wall of nets with mines suspended on them at different heights. He had then got through the Dover nets and entered the Dover Straits. Here, between Folkestone and Cap Gris Nez was another wall of nets and mines allied with sound detector loops which enabled mines to be set off remotely if an unidentified vessel passed by. On the surface, patrols of fast sub-hunter Royal Navy vessels swept the seas. If the sounds of a U-boat were picked up on the detector loops by monitoring stations ashore, these vessels could be directed to the location of the intruder. Giant searchlights swept across the seas. It was a forbidding place for a U-boat, but Lohs was an experienced commander and had run the gauntlet of the British defences many times. He got through without incident and took up a position on the surface, near the Owers Lightship which both the Allies and German U-boats used for navigation. It was common for Allied merchant vessels to pass close to the lightship. In the welcoming cover of darkness, Lohs ordered that the engines be switched off as the U-boat rocked gently on the surface. In the conning tower spotters scanned the horizon with binoculars looking for the tell-tale dark silhouette of their prey.

In the early hours of 23 May, the *Moldavia*'s convoy of five steamships was spotted some way away. It was a big prize – another kill would see Lohs qualify for the title 'ace' with 100,000 tons of Allied shipping sunk. Lohs immediately had the engines started up and started off on the surface in pursuit, cranking *UB-57* up to its maximum speed of 13.4 knots.

Gradually the gap closed on the slower convoy and soon Lohs was manoeuvring into a firing position. He then gave the order to dive. In half a minute *UB-57* had passed from sight and was hidden from observers on the convoy.

During the dive, the convoy, which was zigzagging to avoid torpedo attack, made a turn and as Lohs stabilised *UB-57* at periscope depth and peered through the periscope he found that the lead ship was now heading directly towards him. He ordered a shot from a bow tube and then dived *UB-57*, taking her down to pass underneath the convoy. A muffled explosion told him that his shot had been successful. *UB-57*'s presence had now been revealed and the naval vessels started a pattern of depth-charging runs.

Aboard the *Moldavia*, most of the crew and troops had still been in their hammocks as the first light of dawn had started to lift the night's cloak of darkness. Suddenly the torpedo from *UB-57* exploded in her port side amidships. The explosion could be heard and felt all over the ship. Fifty-six of the American troops, in a compartment immediately aft of the torpedo impact, died instantly. Everyone, even those furthest from the impact, knew there had been a torpedo strike. Crew and troops alike turned out at once, the crew going to their battle stations and the troops making their way to the deck, some in their night gear. There was no panic and a roll call was made.

The *Moldavia* at first continued on her course under her own steam. But then the effect of the tons of water flooding her rent hull started to become clear. Fifteen minutes after the explosion she ground to a wallowing halt. Below decks the ever-searching water flooding into her hull was seeking out new ways to penetrate throughout her entire length.

The *Moldavia* was soon noticeably settling into the water. The sea-level rose inexorably up her sides, water spilling over her decks. The trickling tide of water moving up her main deck turned into a steady stream. Damage reports to Acting Captain A.H. Smyth made it clear that his ship was doomed. The escorting naval vessels were ordered to come alongside *Moldavia* and the crew abandoned ship in an orderly fashion.

Royal Navy destroyers were continuing to depth-charge the scene of the attack to try and catch the silent killer of the *Moldavia*. Everyone was aware that the U-boat might still be close by, watching unseen through a periscope. Indeed there may be more than one U-boat in the vicinity, attracted by the valuable convoy. At any time another torpedo might come slamming into her side as a coup de grace.

The remaining convoy vessels moved on, leaving the *Moldavia* to her fate. She settled further by the head. Her majestic bows disappeared beneath the water, their water-filled weight dragging the front of the ship under and forcing her great stern to lift upwards, her massive twin screws and rudder rising up. She held there, seemingly suspended and motionless, before starting her final descent into the depths. The *Moldavia* slid down into the water by the head and as she did so, jets of steam and air were forced out of her, the sea churning and foaming as she slid under. Finally the water raced up and enveloped her stern and she passed from the sight of the onlookers. The ship plunged down through 150 feet of water, the colossal weight of her water-filled hull picking up speed as she went. She impacted onto the sandy bottom, rolling completely over onto her damaged port side, concealing the area of the torpedo explosion. Her roll to port had probably started on the surface as the water had rushed into the port side of her hull through the torn plating, causing her to list to that side.

Once she had come to a rest on the bottom, the Royal Naval escort vessels dropped a hail of depth charges to try and sink her attacker. The focus of the depth-charging pattern slowly moved away from her wreck. The sounds of the explosions became more muffled and then petered out. The silence of the deep enveloped the *Moldavia*. She was now a prisoner in the liquid world.

THE HAUNTING REMAINS OF THE BRITISH LINER *MOLDAVIA*

UB-57 managed to evade the avalanche of depth charges and make her way away from the scene of the attack. Three days later Lohs would target and sink another vessel also destined to become one of England's greatest shipwrecks, the 6,953-ton steamship *Kyarra*, the focus of Chapter Four.

Today the wreck of the *Moldavia* lies in a general depth of around 50msw although given the tidal range, this depth can be exceeded, particularly around scours at the bow and stern. She lies 26 miles out from Littlehampton at Position 50 23.160 N, 000 28.768 W, far out into the Channel. This far out she is in mid-Channel waters, which are not so badly affected by run-off and pollution as the waters close inshore. Accordingly, divers often find themselves drifting over this fabulous wreck in magnificent underwater visibility of 10-20 metres.

The wreck herself lies on her port side and is orientated north-east/south-west with her bows pointing to the north-east. Her uppermost starboard side and rail are reached at a depth of around 38msw. The most visually haunting sight on this wreck is the huge bow section, which remains completely intact. Her massive straight stem looks as though it is still ready to slice majestically through even the heaviest of seas, although the highest part of the actual stem strip itself has sprung from the framework of the hull.

Both her lower port side and uppermost starboard side massive twin-fluted anchors are still held snugly in their hawse pipes hard against the side of the hull, as they had been for her long transatlantic crossing. The anchor chains run from the anchors back through the hawses onto the now almost vertical main deck. From here they lead back through a steel semi-circular fairlead to a huge circular steam-driven anchor capstan. At either side of the deck here are sited mooring bollards and cleats.

The decking and sections of the ship's hull here and there have rotted away to reveal her ribs, beams and framing. Right next to the capstan, on the centre line of the vessel, is situated a robust rotating crane, its cylindrical arms forming a triangular shape – this was designed for deploying a spare anchor in the event of one of the main anchors being lost or damaged. Interestingly, if the portside photograph of the *Moldavia* at the beginning of this chapter is studied in enough detail, it can be seen that the portside anchor is not in its hawse but is in fact suspended over the portside of the ship from this crane right up at the level of the gunwale. Down below a small boat has three crew members in it who are awaiting the anchor being lowered down to them for shackling to the anchor chain itself, which is run out through the hawse.

Aft of the capstan and crane are situated the foredeck cargo-carrying holds. The foremast itself, which originally stood between these holds at a rakish angle, has fallen from the wreck to the seabed below. Aft of the foredeck holds stood the bridge and central superstructure, which extended aft for some two-thirds of the length of the vessel. At the very front of this superstructure were set saloons and on the higher levels, the navigating bridge, chart rooms, radio room and the captain's quarters, as ever close to the bridge itself, where he might be needed at short notice at any time.

Aft of the bridge itself, the superstructure housed passenger cabins and the engine casing. The two massive funnels passed through this superstructure. At either side of this deckhouse, wooden lifeboats were slung in davits.

Today, this whole superstructure, which was built of lightweight steel and wood, has rotted and collapsed en masse down towards the seabed. The result is a tangled and confused mass of debris, sections of deckhousing, doorways, portholes and the innards of this huge superstructure. The uppermost starboard side of the hull itself has also collapsed downwards, the hull plates being bent over smoothly. Whereas on the uppermost starboard side of the hull at the bow divers will be in a depth of around 40msw, as divers follow the starboard side hull along here they will be dropping down to a depth of 45–50msw. On the uppermost side of the hull here, two rows of portholes dot the side plating, many still with the brass fitment and glass still securely fixed to the hull.

At the end of the collapsed section of hull and superstructure the hull regains its shape and there is a gap where cargo hatches allowed access for loading her aftmost holds. The main mast formerly situated here has, like the foremast, collapsed down to the seabed. One of the most striking features in this area is her uppermost starboard 6-inch gun, the barrel for which points defiantly up towards the distant surface.

Moving further astern the stern deckhouse superstructure is reached. Like the midships superstructure this has largely collapsed downwards. On her uppermost starboard side mooring cleats and bollards can still be made out situated at main deck level, below the uppermost poop deck.

Moving out over her stern it is evident that both her twin 18-foot-diameter propellers have been salvaged. Her massive rudder still sits in place, its gudgeons still secure on the ship's pintles. The rudder itself has rotated downwards so that its outermost end rests on the seabed.

A dive on the wreck of the *Moldavia* is one that most divers will strive for. It is an exciting expedition far out into the Channel. There is no land visible in the distance. The water is a deep 50 metres or more, right at the maximum recommended limit for air diving. All divers diving this wreck on air will be affected by *nitrogen narcosis*, the 'raptures of the depths', to lesser or greater degrees. The *Moldavia* is a dive only for experienced divers who have worked up to diving to this depth. She is a fascinating glimpse back 100 years to a different, elegant era of sea travel. The wreck is massive – its fixtures and fitting, anchors, bollards are all oceangoing size. Everywhere you look on this wreck there is something that will grab your interest, be it the 6-inch guns pointing to the distant surface far above the uppermost starboard side of the wreck, or quite simply, the rarity of seeing portholes with their brass and glass opening lights still in place.

The wreck teems with all sorts of fish and marine life that find both shelter and food in the *Moldavia*'s rotting skeleton. Crabs and lobsters ferret for food in her plates and collapsed superstructure whilst large schools of fish drift over her remains, sometimes in such numbers that her framework is partially obscured. For any decent bottom time on this wreck divers will inevitably have a long ascent profile for decompression before the surface is reached. The time

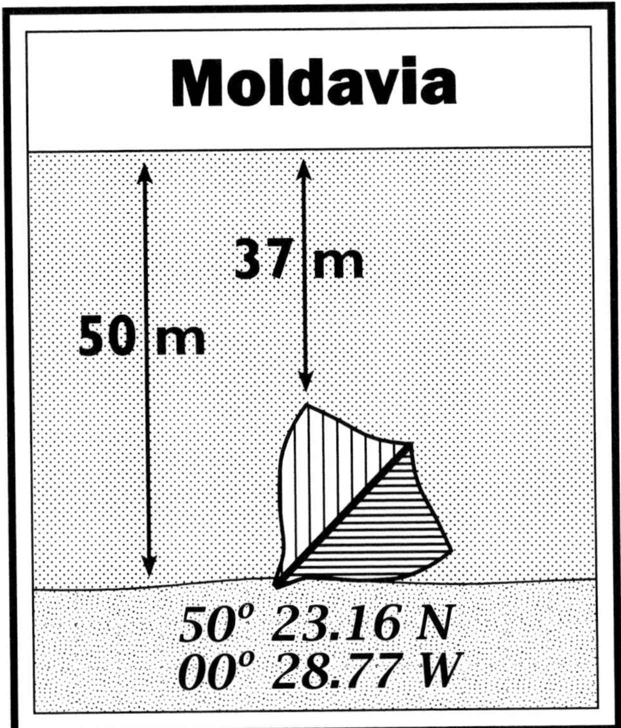

DIVE DETAILS FOR THE BRITISH LINER *MOLDAVIA*

spent decompressing will certainly be worthwhile and will no doubt pass quickly as you recall the highlights of a dive on one of England's greatest wrecks.

ESSENTIAL INFORMATION

BOAT LAUNCH SITE: Being 26 miles offshore, this is a hard boat dive only. Boats go out from Brighton and Littlehampton. Paul and Kelly Childs run the 10m catamaran *Voyager* ex-Littlehampton, and have just taken delivery of a brand new 11m cat, *Defiant* (01903) 739090. Channel Diving (01273) 301142.

TIDAL CONDITIONS: Strongly tidal – dive at slack water only.

VISIBILITY: 10–25 metres.

MAXIMUM DEPTH: 50msw. Slightly more in scour under stern at high water.

LEAST DEPTH: 37msw to upturned starboard rail.

COASTGUARD: Solent Coastguard (02392) 584255.

RECOMPRESSION FACILITIES: Haslar, Gosport (02392) 584255.
AIR SUPPLIES: *Voyager* (above) provide air supplies for their own customers. Wittering Divers Ltd., 185 Portland Road, Hove, Brighton (01273) 737718.
HYDROGRAPHIC CHART: Anvil Point to Beachy Head, No 2450.
POSITION: Lat 50 23.160 N, Long 000 28.768 W.
DIVER LEVEL: Advanced experienced divers only.

Chapter 9

RMS *Alaunia I*, Hastings, East Sussex

The beautiful 520-foot-long Cunard liner *Alaunia I* lies in 35 metres of water off the East Sussex coast. Photo courtesy of www.merseysideviews.com

The 520-foot-long Cunard liner *Alaunia I* is quite simply the largest wreck off the East Sussex coast. Although she is well deteriorated, the wreck remains a tantalising glimpse of a once-majestic oceangoing liner. All her fitments, from massive anchors to bollards, hawses and steering gear are those of a liner, vast in size.

Her bows remain intact, rolled over onto their port side. For divers swimming along her collapsed remains towards the bow, they are an awe-inspiring and imposing sight as they materialise out of the gloom. Lying just a few miles off the coast, she is easily accessed by RIB or hard boat.

Her depth of 30–35msw means that divers can enjoy relatively long bottom times on her as they explore her crumbled remains. You will need that long a dive, for the *Alaunia* is a huge shipwreck indeed. Even though she is now deteriorating and collapsing, her highest point, the upturned starboard rail of her bows, rises up from the seabed at 30-35msw to around 20msw. As a wreck dive she holds something of interest for all levels of diver, be it the thrill of diving such a vast wreck in deep, gloomy water or the sealife that teems around her. She is a wreck that should not be missed.

The *Alaunia* is a relic from the great age of Atlantic sea passenger travel, a time when the Royal Mail Steam Packet Company, the Cunard Line represented the finest and most luxurious way of crossing the Atlantic. The company slogan summed up the prevailing view at the time – 'Getting there is half the fun.'

Founded in 1839 by a resident of Nova Scotia, Mr Samuel Cunard (and originally known as the British and North American Royal Mail Steam Packet Company), the Cunard Line grew from humble beginnings. Realising the early successes of steam ships crossing the Atlantic, Samuel Cunard took a brave gamble and risked his entire fortune. He and 31 other shareholders were able to subscribe the necessary capital to build the first of the Cunard Steamship Company Limited's fleet, the 200-feet long, 32-feet in the beam, wooden paddle steamship, *Britannia*, which was built on the Clyde.

The *Britannia* was launched on 7 February 1840 and set off on its maiden crossing of the Atlantic on 4 July 1840 with Samuel Cunard himself aboard. She was able to complete this voyage in just 12 days and 15 hours.

The construction and acquisition of more ships followed as success was built on success. Although the early ships were constructed from wood, from 1853 onwards all Cunard ships were built of iron and later steel. The new construction promised greater strength and flexibility in shipbuilding and would lead to the development of the more efficient screw propulsion.

In 1869 the rival White Star Line began investing in a line of ships shuttling between New York and Liverpool and started providing competition for the Cunard Line. The White Star ships were large and powerful and incorporated all the huge improvements in shipbuilding design that the ferocious pace of transatlantic shipping was fostering. The two companies would become locked in fierce competition for the next 30 years.

By 1907, the passenger trade had evolved from the spartan *Britannia*, which Charles Dickens had called on its maiden voyage a 'hearse with windows', to large, spacious vessels that catered for unheard-of luxuries at sea. It was in this year that Cunard reached new heights of excellence with the construction of the *Lusitania* by John Brown and Co. Ltd and the *Mauretania* by Messrs Swan, Hunter & Wigham Richardson Ltd. These vast floating palaces were inspired by architectural and decorative styles found on land and mimicked the look of the great London hotels.

The *Alaunia I* itself was built in 1913 in the run-up to the First World War. The Cunard Line had inaugurated its own Canadian service in 1911. The company was aware that it needed its own purpose-built ships for that profitable route. Thus, three vessels were ordered from Scotts Shipbuilding & Engineering Company of Greenock, Glasgow, the *Andania*, the *Alaunia I* and the *Aurania*.

The *Alaunia* was the second of the three ships to be launched, on 9 June 1913. She weighed in at 13,405 tons gross and was fitted out with twin-screw quadruple-expansion engines manufactured by the shipbuilders, which developed 8,500hp, enough to push her and her sister ships to a top speed of 14.5 knots.

The *Alaunia* was constructed of steel with three decks and bridge superstructure, which gave her a total height of 243 feet. She was 540 feet long with a beam of 64 feet. On board was accommodation for 520 second class and 1,620 third-class passengers. The usual third-class dormitories were replaced in this vessel by four- and six-berth cabins. She carried a crew of 289.

The *Alaunia*, *Andania* and *Aurania* were more or less identical vessels. Each was fitted with two masts and each had two towering funnels amidships in the Cunard Line's classic red with black bands at the top.

The *Alaunia* made its maiden voyage on 27 November 1913 from Liverpool to Boston via Queenstown and Portland, arriving in Boston on 6 December 1913. She went on to continue regular Atlantic crossings throughout the first half of 1914 taking emigrants to new lives in America. However, the Great War which was now engulfing Europe caught up with the *Alaunia* in August 1914, when she was requisitioned as a troopship. The *Andania* was requisitioned just two months later in October, also as a troopship.

At this time, arrangements were being made for the transportation of the First Contingent of the Canadian Expeditionary Force to the battlefields of Europe and ships were needed to carry some 25,000 men and the chattels of war across the north Atlantic. Canada, at that time an unmilitary nation, had raised this force in about six weeks following the outbreak of war and now looked for a way to safely send this huge force across the Atlantic. Contracts had been signed by the Minister of Militia, for the acquisition of some 20 ships for this task by 11 September 1914. Initially it was planned to send the troops across in stages but latterly it was decided to send the entire force that had been assembled at Valcartier, Canada, across the Atlantic in one single convoy, which would be heavily protected. Accordingly, the number of ships needed was increased to more than 30.

The *Alaunia* found herself as one of this vast fleet of ships destined to make a dangerous crossing of the Atlantic, where the convoy could be attacked by elements of the powerful and feared German High Seas Fleet and by U-boats. The *Alaunia* was ideal for this task; she was large and reasonably fast, and could easily carry both large numbers of troops and a sizeable cargo.

The designated merchant ships rendezvoused at Montreal where they were prepared for their troopship role. As soon as they were ready they proceeded down the river to Quebec where they were to embark their troops. The process of embarkation began on 23 September. This was a huge undertaking in numbers of ships, men and materials. It took until 1 October before the last ship was finally loaded and ready to set sail.

The total figures for the First Contingent for the Atlantic crossing gives some idea of the scale of the deployment. In all, there were 1,547 officers, 29,070 men, 7,679 horses, 70 field guns, 110 motor vehicles and 705 horsed vehicles. As the loading of each ship at the quayside was completed, that ship would then move out into the river and anchor until the captain received sealed orders to proceed to an anchorage in Gaspé Bay.

A powerful Royal Navy force was assembled to escort and protect the armada. Four cruisers, the pre-dreadnought battleship HMS *Glory*, the Lion class battlecruiser HMS *Princess Royal* and the Majestic class pre-dreadnought, HMS *Magnificent*, were tasked and made their way to Gaspé Bay. A second battleship was scheduled to join the group during the passage across the Atlantic – if the squadron were to be attacked by German ships it would be in the second half of the crossing as they neared Europe.

As the merchant vessels arrived in Gaspé Bay they were anchored in the positions they would hold in the convoy on sailing, in three columns, X, Y and Z.

X	Y	Z
Scotian	*Caribbean*	*Megantic*
Arcadian	*Athena*	*Ruthenia*
Zeeland	*Royal Edward*	*Bermudian*
Corinthian	*Franconia*	***Alaunia***
Virginian	*Canada*	*Ivernia*
Andania	*Monmouth*	*Scandanavian*
Saxonia	*Manitou*	*Sicilian*

Grampian	*Tyrolia*	*Montezuma*
Lakonia	*Tunisian*	*Lapland*
Montreal	*Laurentic*	*Cassandra*
Royal George		*Florizel*

The convoy escorts arranged themselves into formation with the pre-dreadnought HMS *Magnificent* in the lead. The three cruisers HMS *Eclipse*, *Diana* and *Charybdis* each led one of the three columns of merchant vessels. The battlecruiser HMS *Princess Royal* took station on the port wing and the pre-dreadnought HMS *Glory* on the starboard wing. The cruiser HMS *Talbot* took up the rear.

On 3 October 1914 HMS *Charybdis* made the following signal to the troop ships:

> Have cables hove short. All ships in column Z will raise anchor at 3 p.m. and proceed, keeping column formation, steaming at 9 knots following lead cruiser *Eclipse*.

Promptly at 3 p.m. HMS *Eclipse* led column Z out of the anchorage, followed by HMS *Diana* with column Y and in due course, astern of her came HMS *Charybdis* leading column X. HMS *Talbot* brought up the rear. The column of ships stretched out for an incredible 21.5 miles. Even though the ships started to leave the anchorage at 3 p.m., the last ship did not pass the entrance until 6 p.m.

As the powerful convoy with its precious cargo of fighting men and machines proceeded on its way across the Atlantic towards the war in Europe, other war ships were rendezvousing with it and moving into position to shepherd the convoy for disembarkation in Southampton.

Invaluable camp equipment, without which the troops could not be dealt with ashore, was stored in the *Montreal* and *Alaunia* so it was essential that these two ships be unloaded first on arrival in Britain. Accordingly, these two ships, escorted by HMS *Diana* parted company with the rest of the convoy en route, some 570 miles west of Scilly on 11 October.

The following day however, 12 October, a submarine was sighted off Cap Gris Nez towards the eastern end of the English Channel by the French Navy. Then on 13 October, a submarine was sighted and attacked by one of the torpedo boats of the Portsmouth Extended Defence at the east end of the Isle of Wight. The presence of this submarine so near to Southampton made it too dangerous to try to disembark there. Accordingly, the Admiralty ordered the massive convoy to alter course and shelter in Plymouth Sound until the channel to the Needles could be cleared. The same orders were sent to HMS

Diana and the two merchant vessels under her charge, *Montreal* and *Alaunia*. They arrived at Devonport at dawn on 14 October.

It was later learned that the two hostile submarines sighted on 12 and 13 October on the approaches to Southampton had been specially ordered by German command to attack the convoy. German intelligence, however, was slightly flawed as they had understood that the troops aboard the convoy vessels were fully trained and were bound for Boulogne for immediate deployment in theatre. Thus *U-8* and *U-20* were sent to operate off Boulogne. Neither submarine seems to have come so far west as Plymouth, where the convoy vessels would have been detected and threatened. Had the German intelligence not been flawed as to the point of disembarkation for the troop ships, the *Alaunia* and her other merchant vessels would have been in very real danger.

Admiral Jellicoe had made huge preparations on the British side of the Atlantic to try to ensure the safe passage of the vital convoy to Britain. On 3 October the British Grand Fleet had been deployed from its base at Scapa Flow in the Orkney Islands. The Fleet took up strategic positions to ensure that no German warships broke out from the North Sea during the vital week when the convoy approached Britain.

The 1st Battle Cruiser Squadron was tasked to guard the Fair Island Channel and the 2nd Battle Cruiser Squadron was sent to patrol to the north and east of Shetland. The 1st Light Cruiser Squadron along with the 2nd, 3rd and 10th Cruiser Squadrons were also tactically deployed in strategic positions. The Dreadnought Battle Fleet, the 3rd and 6th Battle Squadrons, was also deployed to guard key areas of water with countless destroyers allocated to guard more local approaches. These massive deployments of Royal Navy warships ensured the safety of the convoy, the 30,000 troops and indeed the *Alaunia* herself.

The following year saw the *Alaunia* operating in support of the Gallipoli landings. In April 1915, the Allies decided to launch a fresh attack against the Turks. If the Dardanelle Straits could be captured, Turkey would be cut in two. Britain's ally, Russia, would then have her southern ports open once more and Britain would be able to assist her in an all-out assault on Constantinople where all of Turkey's arms factories were situated. If Constantinople could be smashed, their arms production would soon collapse. Germany would then be without an ally and neutrals tempted to throw in their lot with the Kaiser would think again. The back door to Europe would be open. Suvla Bay, 25 miles north of Cape Helles, was chosen for the assault.

The 10th (Irish) Division, which included the 6th and 7th Battalions of the Royal Dublin Fusiliers, set sail for the Gallipoli landings aboard the *Alaunia* under the command of Captain Rostron. He had sprung to fame three years earlier when he was in command of the *Carpathia* as she came to the rescue of the *Titanic* disaster survivors. Administrative incompetence resulted in the *Alaunia* and her troops initially being sent to France – not Gallipoli. When the *Alaunia* and her troops did eventually arrive in Gallipoli, the troops had neither maps nor orders. They were faced with a chronic water shortage and ran out of ammunition – they even had to resort to throwing stones at the enemy. After disembarking her troops, the *Alaunia* found herself later in 1915 carrying troops to Bombay in India.

In January 1916 the Allies withdrew from Gallipoli. They had not gained any ground, but had suffered some 250,000 casualties. Of the 10th (Irish) Division who had sailed out in the *Alaunia*, 3,411 were dead, wounded or missing.

That same year, 1916, the *Alaunia* returned to the cold North Atlantic to her first wartime role of carrying troops to the European theatre from Canada and America. She was joined on the London to New York run by one of her two original sister ships, the *Andania*. It was in this role that the *Alaunia* left London on 19 September 1916 on a return voyage to New York. Unbeknown to her, the hand of fate was now turning against her, for the return leg of this voyage was to be her last.

On 19 October, having safely crossed the dangerous Atlantic on the return leg, as she headed up the English Channel for London, she was suddenly rocked without warning by an enormous explosion two miles south of the Royal Sovereign Lightship, off Eastbourne, East Sussex. She slewed to a wallowing halt and it soon became clear that she had struck a mine. The alert was put out and rescue vessels got up steam and headed towards her. Being such a sizeable vessel she did not sink immediately. She remained afloat but started to settle slowly into the water. An initial attempt was made to take the ship in tow with tugs and run for shore to beach the vessel and save it. However, the damage caused by the mine explosion proved too severe; the rate of water flooding into her hull was too fast.

The *Alaunia* settled steadily into the water and when it became clear that she was going to founder before the shallows could be reached, the order was given for the ship to be abandoned. All passengers and 163 of the crew were safely taken ashore. Two of the crew, a steward and a trimmer, sadly perished. As she disappeared beneath the dark waters of the Channel, the *Alaunia* made her last voyage, to the bottom of the Channel where she lies today.

The *Alaunia*'s sister ship, *Andania*, also failed to survive the war. She was torpedoed and sunk by a German U-boat to the north of Rathlin Island lighthouse with the loss of seven.

With her valuable non-ferrous machinery and fitments, and lying in relatively

THE MASSIVE REMAINS OF THE *ALAUNIA* LIE IN 35MSW, SEVERAL MILES OFFSHORE FROM EASTBOURNE, EAST SUSSEX. © ROD MACDONALD 2003

shallow waters not far offshore, the wreck of the *Alaunia* attracted the attention of salvers. Her propellers were easy to remove, and holes were blasted in her hull in various places and her cargo removed. After that work was completed the wreck of the *Alaunia* was allowed to rest in peace in the depths of the Channel.

Today the wreck of the once-majestic *Alaunia* lies several miles south of Eastbourne at Position 50 41.087 N, 000 27.184 E. This puts her about 2.4 nautical miles south of the Royal Sovereign Light Tower (50 43.39 N, 00 26.13 E) which stands where the Royal Sovereign Lightship formerly was stationed. She lies in a roughly east-west orientation with her bows pointing to the east.

The Marina at Eastbourne Village is the nearest sea access to the wreck site. The Marina teems with crafts of all shapes and sizes and is surrounded by newly and tastefully constructed blocks of apartments. All around there is new construction in this developing area with large stores, cinemas, and quayside restaurants and bars.

From here there are several dive boats that regularly take dive charters out to the *Alaunia* and the many other wrecks in this area. In the main Marina complex there is conveniently a very good dive shop, Planet Dive, which can provide clean air fills and Nitrox. It is also a TDI (Technical Diving Inc.) facility and so also provides Trimix for the deeper dives.

There is a tidal range of about 6 metres in this area and so a lock system is employed for vessels such as dive boats entering and exiting the Marina. The lock gates open and close regularly every half an hour. Miss the scheduled half-hour opening and you have to wait another 30 minutes for the next.

Once through the lock gates the dive boat heads out to sea. The large sweep of the beach to the east of the Marina stretches out into the distance, but then starts to shrink astern as the bows of the dive boat head seaward.

On the run-out the massive concrete Royal Sovereign Light Tower platform dominates the horizon. Once past the tower, the dive boat is more than halfway out to the last resting place of the *Alaunia*.

Once on site, the boat's echo-sounder trace jumps up from a flat-shelving seabed to reveal the presence of something massive lying on the seabed beneath. A weighted shot line is deployed and sinks quickly to the wreck. Depending on when you dive, the depth to the seabed will be in the region of 30–35msw. It is time for the divers to enter the water.

As the divers splash into the water an explosion of bubbles and white water envelopes them. As the froth disappears they can right themselves and make their way over to the shot line. An exchange of OK signals means it is time for the descent to commence. Each diver dumps the air in his buoyancy wings and dive suit, making him slightly negatively buoyant. The divers start to sink, keeping a watchful eye and hand on the shot line. If they lose contact with the shot line, in the limited visibility of this area of the Channel they will quickly become disorientated and could end up missing the wreck completely.

The waters close over the divers as the descent commences. The topmost parts of the wreck are some 20 metres beneath them. As they move down the shot line their surroundings darken as the plankton and particles in suspension in the water filter out the ambient sunlight trying to penetrate down through the water. It becomes dark, then darker, and then seemingly black. The divers start to feel increasing water pressure on their eardrums. This is easily relieved by 'popping' their ears, as in a plane. The increasing water pressure compresses the air in their dry suits and buoyancy wings, causing discomfort and an increasing rate of descent. If this is not checked they could get into difficulty and so air is bled from their back tanks into their suits, relieving the squeeze and into their wings for buoyancy. They have long since mastered the diver's art of maintaining neutral buoyancy – the equilibrium where they neither sink downwards nor float upwards – in this liquid world.

Suddenly the gloom takes form before their eyes – they have arrived at the highest point, the very bows of the wreck. Although earlier reports of the wreck indicated that the bows were sitting upright with a list to port, the whole bow section, some 75 feet in length, has now rolled onto her port side.

Peering over the remaining struts of the uppermost starboard handrail, the divers can see that the starboard-side anchor and chain have run out from their hawse pipe for a short distance. The starboard-side anchor is now draped over the very keel of the ship itself, hanging loosely suspended on its chain. The divers can follow the anchor chain back to where it is still wrapped round a massive central circular anchor capstan before the chain disappears below decks to the chain locker.

A small hatchway allows access to the foredeck spaces below deck and just beside it, a distinctive triangular derrick and kingpost is still set in the deck, formerly intended for moving heavy pieces of machinery on the foredeck and for deploying the spare anchor should an anchor chain be cut and an anchor lost. On either side of the hull here are set distinctive quad-mooring bollards. The spare anchor itself would originally have been chained on the foredeck but this has now fallen from its mounts as the bow section rolled over and can be found on the seabed just aft of the capstan.

Some 75 feet back from the majestic straight stem of the ship the intact bow section suddenly comes to a halt. The hull appears to have collapsed inwards and divers can spend time exploring the cavernous innards of the huge bow section of hull before moving astern.

The plating aft of the bow section is initially quite flat, with lots of spaces and nooks and crannies hiding all sorts of marine life, such as crabs and lobsters. On the seabed here just projecting from the debris, the massive tubular foremast with its distinctive crow's nest still in place can be seen. A lifeboat davit still stands in place.

Moving further aft it is clear that the whole superstructure of this wreck has been removed, as the hull is open right down to the engine-room area with many of its large fitments such as donkey boilers still in place. At the starboard side of the wreck sections of hull plating are still in situ, with large girders and ribs projecting upwards to give an idea of her original shape. As evidence of the blasting from the salvage work on her, large sections of her

DIVE DETAILS FOR THE *ALAUNIA*

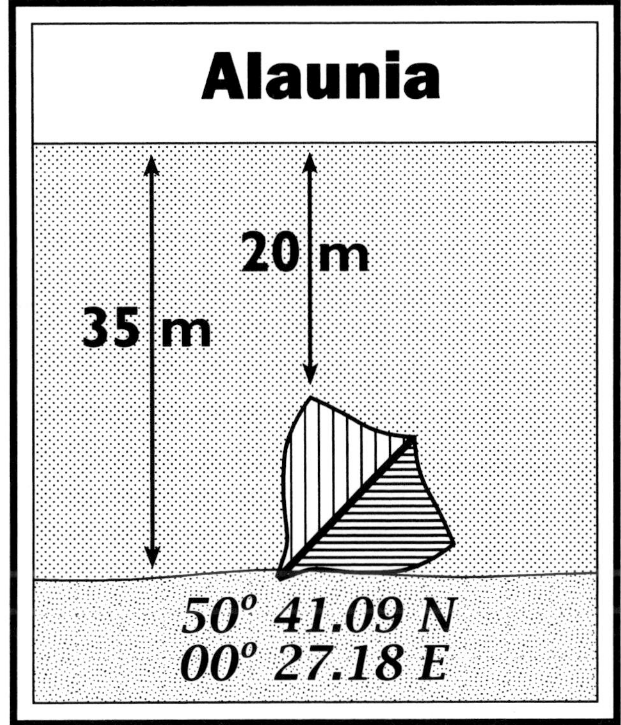

uppermost plating with rows of portholes and doorways lie at right angles across the wreck. Where the plating ends, dark, ominous holes allow a glimpse into her innards. At her starboard side sections of her double bottom project upwards.

Aft of this area the prop shaft emerges from its tunnel and leads dead astern down the centre of the wreck as large sections of torn plating and ribs project upwards at either side. The divers have now passed beyond the location of the original superstructure and are in the vicinity of the aft holds. The main deck here has collapsed down so that several large winches originally used for working a derrick system to load and unload her holds have now fallen through the wreck and lie athwartships over the prop shaft itself. A section of one of the hatches for an aft hold helps to keep divers orientated on the wreck.

Further astern, both sides of the ship seem to have collapsed inwards, giving the wreck a narrowing, thin feel. The ship, however, soon opens up again at the very stern, with large sections of the ship's side and ribs sticking up from the debris. The one feature that dominates this area is a massive steering quadrant which stands clear and high of the wreckage. Aft of that the stern is reached.

This wreck is so huge that divers will use up all their available bottom time making this one tour the length of the ship. There is no chance of them making it all the way back to the shot line at the bow to ascend. The divers will deploy delayed decompression buoys on reels. When these large red or yellow bags, or 6-foot-tall sausage buoys, reach the surface they instantly tell the dive boat skipper that the divers have started their ascent. Depending on the dive profile, they will be carrying out decompression stops as they make the slow ascent to the surface. The skipper will follow the deco bags as the divers hang free, drifting in the prevailing current until it is time for them to exit the water. On the next dive they can choose the particular area that caught their interest and perhaps spend the whole dive exploring that one section in depth. The wreck of the *Alaunia* is huge and exciting. It is one that divers will need several dives to appreciate in full.

Essential Information

BOAT LAUNCH SITE: Eastbourne Marina.

HARD BOAT DIVING: Taurus Dive Charters, Eastbourne, have a good hard boat which takes divers out to this wreck. (07860) 934712. MV *Sussex*, Eastbourne, (0208) 407 9407, www.sussexshipwrecks.co.uk. Channel Diving (01273) 301142. *Spartacat* (01273) 586445, www.spartacat.co.uk

TIDAL CONDITIONS: This wreck should only be dived at slack water as it is very tidal.

VISIBILITY: During May the Channel experiences a plankton bloom, the May Waters, which drops visibility to just a few metres. Diving later in the summer, the visibility will be 5–15 metres.

MAXIMUM DEPTH: 30–35msw depending at what state of the tide the wreck is dived. Tidal range of approximately 6 metres.

LEAST DEPTH: 20msw on higher starboard side of bows.

COASTGUARD: East Sussex Coatguard (01304) 210008.

RECOMPRESSION FACILITIES: Haslar, Gosport (02392) 584255.

AIR SUPPLIES: Planet Dive, Sovereign Harbour, Eastbourne (01323) 472126. Air to 300 bar, Nitrox and Trimix available.

HYDROGRAPHIC CHART: Beachy Head to Dungeness, No 536.

POSITION: Lat 50 41.087 N, Long 000 27.184 E.

DIVER LEVEL: Given the depth and sometimes poor underwater visibility this wreck is for experienced divers only and not for novices.

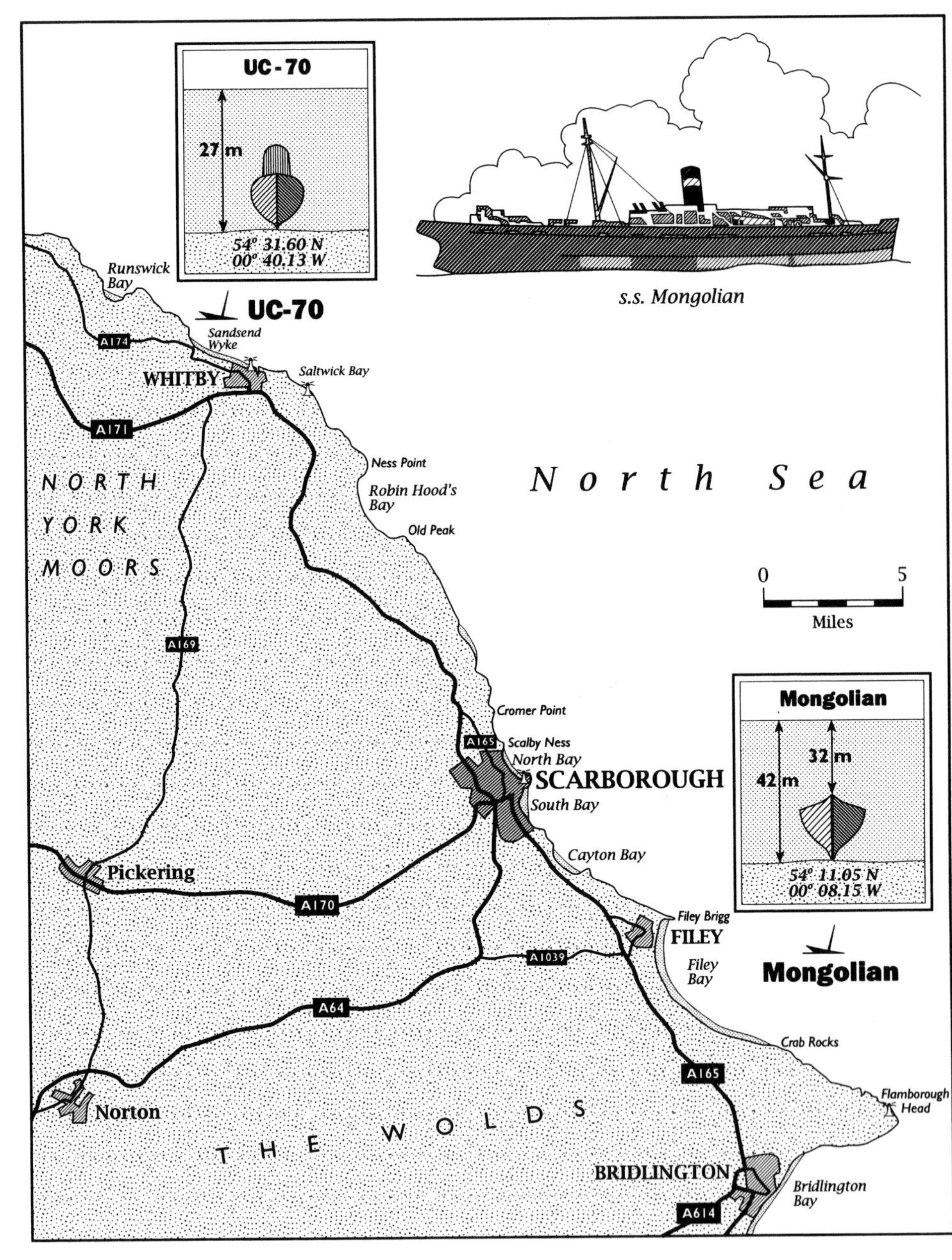
UC-70
27 m
54° 31.60 N
00° 40.13 W
s.s. Mongolian
Runswick Bay
UC-70
Sandsend Wyke
A174
WHITBY
Saltwick Bay
A171
Ness Point
Robin Hood's Bay
Old Peak
North Sea
NORTH YORK MOORS
0
5
Miles
A169
Cromer Point
A165
Scalby Ness
North Bay
SCARBOROUGH
South Bay
Mongolian
32 m
42 m
54° 11.05 N
00° 08.15 W
Cayton Bay
Pickering
A170
Filey Brigg
FILEY
Filey Bay
Mongolian
A1039
A64
Crab Rocks
A165
Flamborough Head
Norton
THE WOLDS
BRIDLINGTON
Bridlington Bay
A614

OPPOSITE: LOCATION CHART FOR WRECKS OF SS *MONGOLIAN* AND *UC-70*

CHAPTER 10

SS *MONGOLIAN*, FILEY BAY, YORKSHIRE

THE 4,838-GROSS-TON SS *MONGOLIAN* UNDERWAY IN PORT. NOTE THE FOREMAST RIGGED FOR SAIL. PHOTO COURTESY OF THE NATIONAL MARITIME MUSEUM, GREENWICH

The Yorkshire coast of England saw a huge number of shipping losses during both world wars of the twentieth century. The many heavy industries of the major east coast cities meant that shipping between the ports and down to London was very prolific. During the First World War, small coastal U-boats were specifically tasked to operate around the entrances to these ports, striking unsuspecting merchant ships with torpedoes or laying mine barrages.

During the Second World War a channel, regularly swept

for mines, ran from London all the way up to the Orkney Islands of north Scotland just a few miles offshore, marked by buoys. Further out to sea the swept channel was protected by the great Northern Mine Barrage. Nevertheless U-boats were able to slip through the Barrage and wreak havoc with their deadly cargo of mines and torpedoes. In addition German planes ranged over the North Sea from bases in Norway and many ships were lost to bombing. The Admiralty Charts of this coast are littered with innumerable wreck symbols.

Nearly 60 years after the end of the Second World War it is difficult for those of us who have never experienced war on this scale to take in and appreciate the full meaning and horror of what the charts with their simple wreck symbols mean. The wreck of the SS *Mongolian* in Filey Bay, Yorkshire, is but one of these countless wreck symbols. Each and every one has a gripping story attached to it, of an attack, an explosion, fear, bewilderment and terror, followed by panic and a ship abandoned.

The dramatic story of the sinking of the SS *Mongolian* stands out, however, amidst all these tales as perhaps one of the most ironic. She was sunk by a torpedo from a German submarine, *UC-70*, which was herself to be sunk by the RAF just a few months later off Whitby, not far to the north of Filey Bay. Once the hunter, *UC-70* had become the prey. The hunter submarine and the hunted SS *Mongolian* now lie in their watery coffins in the uncaring silence of the depths, in relatively close proximity. Young sailors of both sides met their end in the cold dark waters of the Yorkshire coast. The sea was a common enemy that made no distinction between the two sides of this human conflict.

The 4,838 gross ton single screw-steel steamship *Mongolian* was built for the Allan Line Steamship Company Limited of Glasgow, by D. & W. Henderson Ltd, shipbuilders, Glasgow in Partick in 1891. She was a sizeable 400 feet in length with a beam of 45 feet 2 inches and a depth of hold of 30 feet 6 inches. Her net tonnage was 3,088 and her international code letters M.B.S.W.

The *Mongolian*'s coal-fired triple-expansion engines developed a powerful 600hp. Notwithstanding, she had been built at a time when the transition from sail to steam had not been fully and completely made. As a consequence, she was fitted out with two towering masts rising up some 100 feet, the foremast being rigged for sail as a tall ship when needed to supplement her engines.

The *Mongolian* was built with the classic straight stem of her era and raised f'c'stle at the bow. On the f'c'stle deck, one deck above the main deck, was situated her anchor winches with attendant chains rising up from chain lockers below and running out to hawse pipes at either side of the hull.

Aft of the f'c'stle were her foredeck holds with her towering foremast situated in between with its attendant derricks and deck-mounted cargo winches. Above these were set the horizontal yards for her sails.

Aft of these holds stood the central main superstructure that housed the bridge complex and captain's accommodation, with passenger saloons and cabins ranged along the long, low superstructure. Wooden lifeboats hung in their davits atop. The towering single funnel, with the single broad white band of her shipping line, rose up through this superstructure. Being coal-fired, when she was under way, her boilers devouring coal fed by stokers deep within the bowels of the ship, she belched large tell-tale clouds of black smoke. To the rear of this superstructure were situated further cargo holds with her main mast situated in between. At her very stern a small poop deck superstructure gave further accommodation and storage space with two more wooden lifeboats swung in davits above.

The *Mongolian* had a long and varied career at sea of 27 years, in a variety of roles and incarnations, before the torpedo from *UC-70* blasted into her and sent her to the bottom of Filey Bay.

The Allan Line, which ordered her construction, more properly known as the Montreal Ocean Steamship Company, was founded in 1854 and began sailing in 1855 from Britain to Canada. At that time, fares outwards from Britain to Canada were 18 guineas; the return journey was 80 dollars. Sailings from Quebec to Britain were at 9 a.m. every alternate Saturday. Departures from Britain were from Liverpool on Wednesdays.

The Allan Line was thus long established in transatlantic voyaging by the time that the newly constructed SS *Mongolian* joined the fleet in 1891. She was soon put to work on the Liverpool to Quebec run, often starting her journey at Glasgow before travelling to Liverpool to collect more passengers prior to heading out through the North Channel between Ireland and Scotland for the passage across the Atlantic to New York and Quebec.

The main bulk of her passengers were emigrants fleeing poverty for a new life in America or Canada. Regulations by the Secretary of the Treasury of the United States required the delivery of Manifests to the Commissioners of Immigration by the Commanding Officer of any vessel that had passengers on board when it arrived at a port in the United Sates. The regulations required a lot of personal information on each and every passenger, included the following: name; age; sex; marital status; calling or occupation; whether the passenger was able to read or write; nationality of passenger; last residence; final destination: state, city or town; whether a ticket was held for that final destination; by whom was the passage paid; whether the passenger possessed thirty dollars or more; whether the passenger had ever been in prison before;

physical condition; and whether the passenger was a polygamist.

Many of the *Mongolian*'s Manifests are available on the Internet and reading the personal details of her passengers gives a fascinating insight into the tide of humanity that was crossing the Atlantic in search of a new life at the time. Her passengers were miners, ranchers, farm labourers and the like with many unaccompanied women with children travelling to meet husbands who presumably had gone out some time previously to find employment and settle. These Manifests simply state 'Going to husband'.

The ship's surgeon was personally required to examine each passenger as he/she boarded to try and screen any passengers who were carrying a 'loathsome or dangerous contagious disease' amongst other conditions and affidavits to this effect by the commanding officer and surgeon were delivered along with the Manifests to the Commissioner of Immigration on landing. Not surprisingly, in none of the Manifests did I see any passenger confirm that he/she was indeed a polygamist.

Most of these passengers were brave souls from all over Britain and Europe, giving up all that they knew in the Auld Country for a new life that promised so much – but which very often failed to live up to the dream. The *Mongolian* tirelessly crossed and recrossed the Atlantic with its human cargo from 1891 onwards – becoming a regular and well-known ship on the crossing.

In a now almost forgotten chapter of British history, more than 100,000 British children, the so-called 'Home Children', were packed off by their parents, driven by poverty, between 1870 and 1930 to work on Canadian farms. Many of these children travelled on the *Mongolian*, tagged and shipped as a human cargo bound for farmers in Canada – and destined never to see their mothers and fathers again. At this distance in time it is hard to take in and truly appreciate how dire the financial circumstances must have been that would force a family to be split up in this fashion.

Travelling in groups of up to 400, with their worldly possessions in small trunks, they travelled to what they thought was a land of plenty. Once ashore, they found themselves arriving on foreign railway platforms with their name tags round their necks, to be met by unknown farmers. On 27 May 1913, the records show that a party of 110 Home Children from a single institution, the Middlemore Home in Liverpool, sailed on the *Mongolian* for Halifax.

In the years following the *Titanic* disaster, more accurate reporting of ice and icebergs by vessels resulted in detailed ice charts becoming available for mariners. Being such a regular crosser of the Atlantic to America and Canada, the *Mongolian* made frequent reports of ice and icebergs – her name surfaces often in the reports from the North Atlantic. These ice charts reveal just how large and frequent a threat ice was in the days when the navigational instruments and radar that we take for granted now were not available. The only way of avoiding an iceberg was by spotting it and taking evasive action early enough. Some of the *Mongolian*'s reports give an idea of what a winter crossing of the Atlantic entailed:

> *17 February 1913*: 'Entered fields of slob ice in streaks running north and south.'
> *18 February*: 'Cleared the ice.'
> *20 February*: 'Entered ice 1–18 inches thick extending in a NE and SW direction.'
> *21 February*: 'Cleared the ice.'

Then, later that year:

> 16 April: 'Saw two large ice bergs, 60–70 feet high and numerous growlers.'
> 17 April: 'Encountered ice extending in all directions; dense fog continuing, stopped ship for 36 hours close to ice field.'
> 18 April: 'Two dangerous growlers and a large berg.'
> 19 April: 'Large berg.'

In about 1915, the *Mongolian*'s master, Captain J.W. Hatherly, was tragically killed in an accident aboard the ship whilst she was in harbour in Canada. That same year, *Mongolian*'s owners, the Montreal Ocean Steamship Company, went on to merge with Canadian Pacific Line, the merged company being known as Canadian Pacific Ocean Services Limited. At this time in 1915, the *Mongolian* itself was sold to the British Admiralty. Three years later, in July 1918, the *Mongolian* found herself berthed in the northern port of Middlesbrough being loaded with a general cargo destined for the Italian government. The first leg of her voyage would take her down the east coast of England to London.

On 21 July 1918, her bunkers full of coal, the *Mongolian*'s stokers, deep in the bowels of the ship, worked up a head of steam. She was ready for sea. The command was given and her mooring lines were cast off. She nudged out into the River Tees before moving out into Tees Bay. Moving farther out to sea, she swung to the south, heading for the deeper water of the North Sea. Her scheduled route would take her down the east coast southwards, a few miles offshore, with the land on her starboard beam.

As the *Mongolian* steamed southwards she was unaware that hidden in the dark, silty waters ahead of her, the German submarine *UC-70* was on the loose and scavenging for prey. As she headed south at about 10 knots, Whitby soon passed by on the *Mongolian*'s starboard beam. Shortly after, Scarborough hove into view and passed by.

UC-70 of the Second Flanders Flotilla, based in Zeebruge, was a small U-boat of just 417 tons and some 49 metres in length. She was fitted with two forward-facing torpedo tubes and one aft-facing tube. These tubes were fitted outside the pressure hull itself and hence the tubes could not be reloaded underwater. This was because the main role of *UC-70* was as a mine-laying submarine. She carried a formidable cargo of 18 mines that were loaded in dock into six tubes running fore and aft along the forward section of her hull. These could be deployed in close proximity to each other, sowing a deadly minefield.

Small U-boats such as *UC-70* were designed to operate in shallow coastal waters laying minefields across the entrances to enemy ports and coastal shipping lanes. *UC-70*'s torpedo tubes were loaded and ready to use should any other worthwhile prey pass before her. It was in just such unfortunate circumstances that the doomed *Mongolian* would cross her path.

The tell-tale plume of black smoke from the approaching *Mongolian*'s single smoke stack probably first alerted *UC-70* to the possibility of a kill. The slow, old and large profile of the *Mongolian* made her an easy target. A torpedo from *UC-70* was loosed and blasted into her port side in the vicinity of her boiler-room. In a split second her hull had been ripped open to the sea. Cold, green sea water poured into her innards, immediately altering her trim and forcing her engines out of operation. She slewed to a wallowing halt and started to settle steadily into the water.

The order to abandon ship was given and the wooden lifeboats were swung out from their davits above her large central superstructure, and lowered. As her crew abandoned ship they knew that many of their shipmates had been lost in the torpedo strike. When a final headcount was made it was found that 36 of her crew had perished.

As the waters closed over the trusty old *Mongolian* her two towering masts were the last visible sign of her presence above the waves. They too soon disappeared beneath the waves and she plunged down through 40 metres of cold dark water, eventually impacting into the seabed. The cruel war had claimed another victim.

The *Mongolian* was destined to lie in the dark depths of Filey Bay largely undisturbed. Initially her two towering masts must have reached nearly to the surface and she was no doubt wire-swept to bring them down and reduce the danger to shipping. She was an old ship with an unimportant cargo and was not worthy of commercial salvage. Even her propeller was steel and of no salvage value. The world moved on, and the war to end all wars was halted with the Armistice, to be followed seven months later by the Treaty of Versailles. The *Mongolian* now found herself adopting yet another role at sea, one never envisaged by her makers. Her wreck became colonised by sealife and started a transformation into an artificial underwater reef. Her old metal started to corrode throwing off her thick layers of paint. The thin steel and wooden walls of her superstructure were turned to dust by the sea revealing the skeleton of her framework. The carnage of the Second World War soon once again enveloped the world with more inhumanity and countless other ships found that their destiny also lay at the bottom of the sea. All the while the *Mongolian* rested in the grip of the sea in the depths of Filey Bay, her plates perhaps echoing to the sounds of the new world conflict.

After seeing the *Mongolian* sink, *UC-70* went on to return safely from her patrol to her base in Zeebruge. The following month, on 21 August 1918, *UC-70*, under the command of Oberleutnant Karl Dobberstein, left Zeebruge for yet another patrol in the Whitby area. On 28 August 1918 she successfully attacked and sank the 1,100-ton steamship *Giralda* off Runswick just a few miles north of Whitby, her familiar hunting ground. Six of her crew were lost, the remaining 13 being rescued.

The *Giralda* was, however, the last vessel to be sunk by *UC-70*, for later that same day the hunter submarine would herself become the hunted. It is thought that *UC-70* had suffered some damage in a new British minefield and was sitting on the bottom effecting repairs. Her commander perhaps did not know that she was leaking oil that was rising to the surface and revealing her presence.

At 3 p.m. Pilot Lieutenant Arthur Waring of 246 Squadron RAF had taken off in a Blackburn Kangaroo bomber from Seaton Carew, near Hartlepool, with a 920-lb bomb load. Soon afterwards, at 3.30 p.m., he spotted a long track of oil on the shimmering calm sea off Whitby. As he followed the oil slick it led him to a long, dark silhouette lying stationary on the seabed, the unmistakable shape of a U-boat. Perhaps aware of the loss of the *Giralda* close by earlier that day, Waring turned his Blackburn Kangaroo bomber into an attacking run, dropping a 520-lb bomb at the stationary U-boat and scoring a hit. The sea frothed with the power of the resulting explosion and more oil was seen to gush to the surface.

The destroyer HMS *Ouse*, nearby, saw and heard the explosion and closed in on the scene for the kill, guided by Lieutenant Waring with flares. Once at the scene, HMS *Ouse* dropped ten depth charges at the centre of the dark silhouette and this attack caused more oil and air to rise up from the depths. One can only imagine the scene in the U-boat as her pressure hull was breached and water rushed in. The doomed crew must have struggled for a last breath as the water

THE REMAINS OF THE SS *MONGOLIAN* LIE IN THE DARK DEPTHS OF FILEY BAY, YORKSHIRE. © ROD MACDONALD 2003

finally flooded the entire hull. The lights would very quickly have gone out and in the darkness and shocking cold water inside the U-boat they would have struggled to try and find a way out. The air would have disappeared from the hull as the crewmen held their breath, thrashing about in their panicked death throes. But they could not hold their breath forever. Eventually the breathing reflex, programmed into humans by evolution aeons ago, would overcome them. They would gasp for a breath of air that was not there. Their lungs would fill up with water and slowly the struggling would stop – to be replaced by a deadly calm and silence.

A fortnight later Royal Navy divers located and entered the U-boat, identifying it as *UC-70* – and then the relentless war moved on and she was forgotten about.

Today, the wreck of the once-proud steamship *Mongolian* lies in 35–40msw just a few miles offshore from Filey Bay. The wreck was discovered by a team of local divers in 1973–4 who learned of an unidentified wreck in the location from local fishermen. The team of Alan Davis, John Adams, Arthur Godfrey and Peter Lassey started diving the wreck using wet suits and twin sets. Very quickly they realised that they were diving the remains of a huge shipwreck and within two or three dives located the bell, sitting upright at the front of the f'c'stle. Once the bell was cleaned up the name *Mongolian* was revealed. The identity of the wreck had been confirmed and they could now research its history.

To dive the *Mongolian* small boats can either be launched from the beach at Cobble Landing on the northern section of the breakwater or alternatively from a small slip at Flamborough Head, not far away. The beach is well suited to RIB launching and is used regularly by local divers. Care must be taken as in the summer months the beach is very busy with holidaymakers and bathers and launching restrictions apply.

Filey is a delightful small English coastal resort that still retains a lot of its character and colour. The town centre is full of small shops, hotels and B&Bs, nothing on the grand scale that tends to rob a town of its individuality. The town centre, railway station and shops are all just a few minutes walk away from the beach that dominates Filey and for which it is justly famous.

Filey Bay itself unfortunately seems to be something of a natural trap for sediment and so the underwater visibility to be expected down on the wreck is not usually very good. Local divers talk of average visibility of a silty 2–3 metres with best visibility being around 10 metres. Interestingly, the underwater visibility round the southern side of the Flamborough headland is consistently far better. The wreck lies some 5.5 miles out of Filey Bay and so it is a short ride of some 15–25 minutes out in a RIB to the wreck site. Being such a large wreck, it is an easy target to identify on an echo sounder and to hook into.

The general depth to the seabed varies from 35–44msw depending on when you are diving and what section of the wreck you are at. There is a noticeable scour around the bow and stern. The wreck itself sits on an even keel, with her bows pointing south towards Flamborough Head – still heading in the direction of her final destination, London.

The stern section of the wreck with its schooner stern is perhaps the most intact section of the wreck. Local divers talk in awe of standing on the seabed at 40msw underneath the overhanging stern, and seeing it silhouetted against the faint glimmer of light filtering down from the distant surface. The immensity of the construction of this vessel can then be appreciated as, rising up from the seabed, it is a full 10 metres before divers reach the underside of the stern. Talking

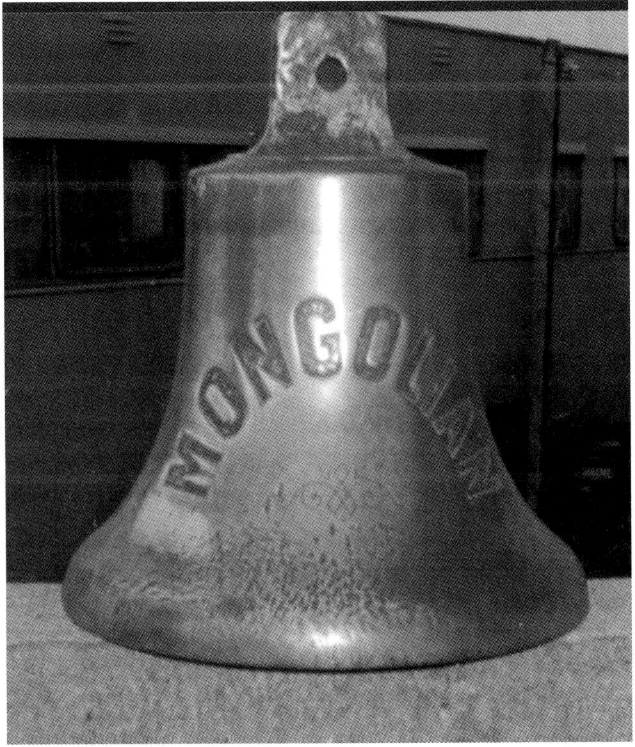

THE BELL OF THE *MONGOLIAN* WAS RECOVERED IN THE 1970S AND ENABLED THE IDENTIFICATION OF THE WRECK. © ALAN DAVIS

to local divers over a few pints in one of the local bars they spoke of the *Mongolian* in terms of being the 'most majestic' wreck in these parts. The rudder is still in position, as is the steel propeller, which was not worthy of salvage.

Moving forward from the stern it becomes clear that the central midships superstructure housing the bridge, passenger cabins and the engine casing and funnel has all but disappeared, turned to dust by the sea. Only a few stronger struts and spars are left sticking up. The hull plating amidships on the port side has collapsed. This is the area where the fateful torpedo struck her. The engine-room has been opened up, making her triple-expansion engine visible, and her massive boilers have been displaced by the force of the explosion amidships. Both of her huge masts have been brought down, presumably by a wire sweep.

The bow area is traditionally one of the strongest areas in a ship as it is designed to withstand the impact of a head-on collision. The bow of the *Mongolian* has thus survived the

DIVE DETAILS FOR SS *MONGOLIAN*

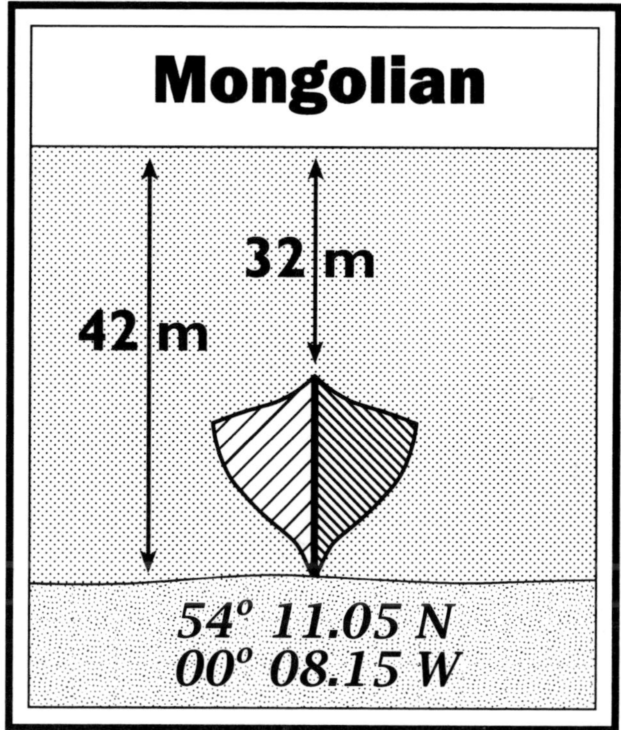

ravages of nearly 90 years immersion better than the central section of the wreck but even it too is now starting to collapse.

The bell of the *Mongolian* subsequently changed hands and now rests in the Steamship Inn in Nottingham. The massive helm of the *Mongolian* was also recovered and raised and is now displayed at Scarborough Sub Aqua Club's base adjacent to the Leeds Arms.

The remains of *UC-70* lie on the seabed just three miles from Whitby Harbour in 27 metres of water. Whitby itself is about 40 minutes' drive north of Filey Bay.

UC-70 is an atmospheric dive on a relatively intact First World War U-boat. She sits on her keel although her conning tower has collapsed to the port side. The dominant feature of the forward section of her hull is the row of six minelaying tubes running fore and aft. Behind them stands her impressive 88mm gun, still facing dead ahead, locked in its travelling position.

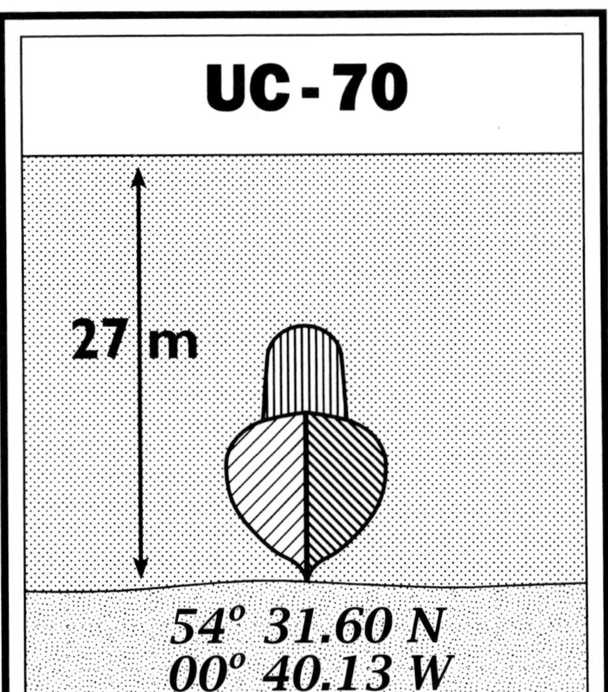

DIVE DETAILS FOR *UC-70*

Just forward of the 88mm gun's barrel, the foredeck hatch from the pressure hull is open – an ominous black hole allowing divers a glimpse of how small and tight this U-boat was. The stern section of the hull also has a corresponding open hatch into the pressure hull. These hatches were presumably opened by the RN divers who dived on the wreck after its initial sinking to identify which U-boat had been sunk.

The wrecks of the *Mongolian* and *UC-70* are a unique time capsule – a single largely forgotten episode of a war ended long ago. The *Mongolian* is the massive leviathan sunk by a torpedo from her smaller but deadly adversary. There is a gripping irony in the tale of how the hunted and the hunter came to lie in the same area of sea so soon after each other – both victims of a cruel war.

ESSENTIAL INFORMATION

BOAT LAUNCH SITE: RIBs can beach launch at Cobble Landing on the north side of the breakwater or from the small slip at Flamborough.

HARD BOAT DIVING: Tony Pockley takes divers and angling parties out to this wreck and others in the locality (01262) 671476.

TIDAL CONDITIONS: Dive at slack water.

VISIBILITY: Average 2–3 metres. Best visibility 10 metres.

MAXIMUM DEPTH: 42msw to seabed.

LEAST DEPTH: 32msw to main deck.

COASTGUARD: Humber Coastguard (01262) 672317.

AIR SUPPLIES: Filey Bay BSAC have a compressor which they are happy to use for visiting divers. Contact David Hunter on (01723) 515780.

HYDROGRAPHIC CHART: Whitby to Flamborough Head, No. 129.

POSITION: SS *Mongolian* – Lat 54.11.048 N, Long 000 08.153 W.
UC-70 – Lat 54.31.598 N, Long 000 40.131 W.

DIVER LEVEL: This is a deep, dark and often low-visibility dive and is for experienced divers only.

BIBLIOGRAPHY

Aspinall-Oglander, Brigadier-General C., *Military Operations, Gallipoli* (London, 1929) (official history)

Burt, R., *British Battleships of the First World War* (London, 1986)

Corbett, Sir Julian and Newbolt, Sir Henry, *History of the Great War: Naval Operations* (London, 1920–31) (official history)

Davis, H.W.C., *A History of the Blockade* (London, 1920)

Duguid, Colonel A. Fortesque, *Official History of the Canadian Forces in the Great War* (King's Printer, Ottawa, 1938)

Gibson, R.H. and Prendergast, M., *The German Submarine War 1914–18* (London, 1931)

Godfrey, Arthur and Lassey, Peter, *Dive Yorkshire* (Underwater World Publications, London, 1988)

Hargrave, J., *The Suvla Bay Landing* (London, 1964)

Haythornthwaite, Philip J., *The World War One Source Book* (Brockhampton Press, London, 1992)

Hinchcliffe, John and Vicki, *Dive Dorset* (Underwater World Publications, 1999)

Hough, R., *The Great War at Sea 1914–18* (Oxford, 1983)

James, R.R., *Gallipoli* (London, 1965)

Jellicoe, Admiral, *The Grand Fleet 1914–16* (Cassel and Co., 1919)

McDonald, Kendall, *Great British Wrecks*, Vol. 1 (Underwater World Publications, London, 1986)

McDonald, Kendall, *Great British Wrecks*, Vol. 2 (Underwater World Publications, London, 1986)

McDonald, Kendall, *Dive South Devon* (Underwater World Publications, London, 1982)

Pullen, Rear-Admiral Hugh, RCN, *Speech from Troop Convoy: How Canada Went to War in 1914* (Crowsnest, 1964)

Salsbury, John, *Sussex Shipwrecks* (West Press Publishing, 1984)

Shovlar, Steve, *Dorset Shipwrecks* (Freestyle Publications, Poole, 1996)

Siney, M.C., *The Allied Blockade of Germany 1914–18* (Ann Arbor, Michegan, 1957)

Stern, Robert C., *Type VII U-boats* (Brockhampton Press, London, 1991)

Taffrail (Captain H. Taprell Dorling), *Swept Channels: Minesweepers in the Great War* (London, 1938)

Tennent, A.J., *British Merchant Ships Sunk by U-boats in the 1914–1918 War* (Starling Press, 1990)

Magazines and Periodicals

Diver magazine:
Wreck Tour 1: The *Maine*, March 1999
Wreck Tour 21: The *Bretagne*, November 2000
Wreck Tour 7: The *Hood*, September 1999
Wreck Tour 11: The *Salsette*, January 2000

Daily Mail
Swanage Times

Websites

www.ssbretagne.co.uk
www.basac.co.uk
UK diving Wreck Database, www.ukdiving.co.uk
www.uboat.net
www.liswa.wa.gov.au/images
www.greatwar.ie/ire_batmb.html
www.merseysideviews.com
www.ku.edu/~kansite/ww_one/naval/1cdncvy.htm
www.uncommonjourneys.com/pages/lines/cunard.htm
www.readingbsac.org.uk

INDEX

DIVE SCAPA FLOW

Rod Macdonald

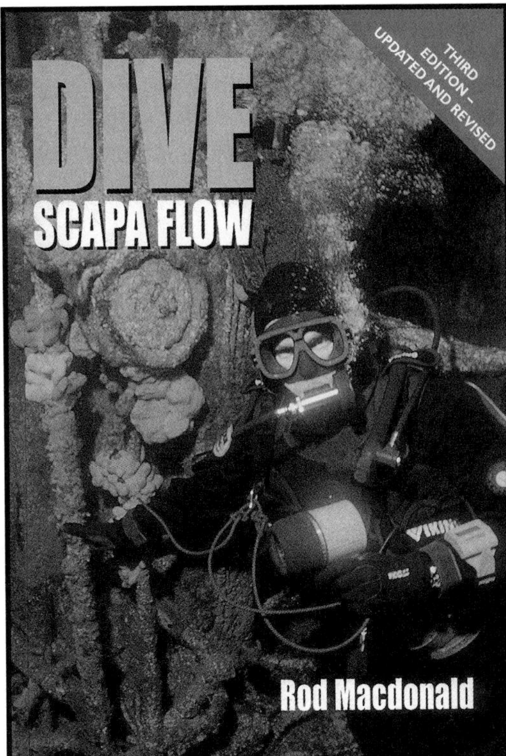

ISBN 1 85158 983 X
£14.99 (ppc)
Now available
240 x 168mm
176pp
1 x 8pp colour, b/w illustrations throughout
Leisure

Dive Scapa Flow is a comprehensive guide to the spectacular Orkney wrecks of the scuttled German fleet. The author uses a mixture of historical narrative of the scuttling and the subsequent salvage to relay the dramatic events at the end of the First World War. This revised edition includes many photographs and details much deeper wrecks reached with the advent of 'technical diving', and it is supplemented by up-to-date information on charters, travel and accommodation.

'A very informative and well-produced publication. A brilliant guide for divers and historians alike, and a bargain at £14.99'
The Nautical Magazine

DIVE SCOTLAND'S GREATEST WRECKS

Rod Macdonald

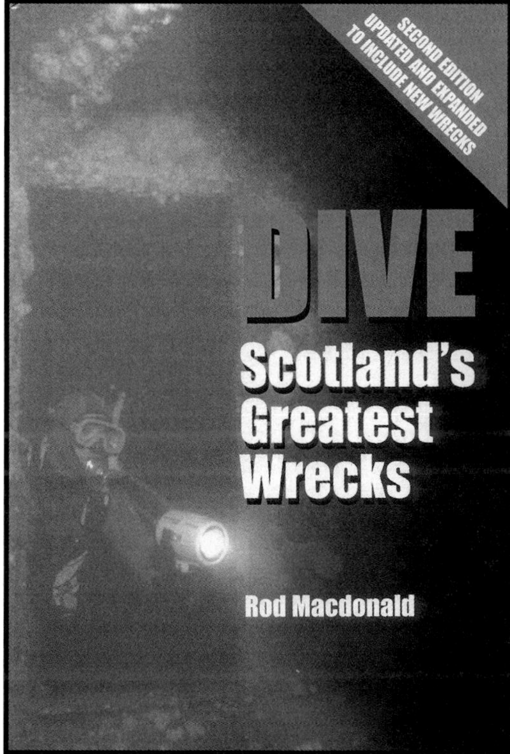

ISBN 1 84018 334 9
£14.99 (ppc)
Now available
240 x 168mm
176pp
1 x 8pp colour, b/w
illustrations throughout
Leisure

Dive Scotland's Greatest Wrecks is a practical and authoritative guide to ten of Scotland's most famous shipwrecks, carefully selected by accomplished diver Rod Macdonald. The story of the sinking of each vessel is dramatically recounted and accompanied by a detailed description of the wreck as it lies today. Each wreck is brought to life by specially commissioned illustrations and the dives are depicted with charts and underwater photographs that enable the reader to experience the sunken treasures beneath Scotland's coastal waters.

'Another enjoyable read from the pen of Rod Macdonald'
Scottish Diver

SCOTS AND THE SEA

James D.G. Davidson

ISBN 1 84018 694 1
£15.99 (hardback)
May 2003
234 x 156mm
256pp
1 x 8pp b/w
History

With over 6,000 miles of rugged coastline and seven major seaports, it is no wonder that the sea has shaped Scotland and that Scots have helped to shape maritime history, trade and communications.

Scots and the Sea is a unique and compelling account of this continuing interaction. It details the origins of Scotland's maritime traditions, the founding of a Scottish merchant navy, the pressures towards Union, development of trade, ports, harbours, shipbuilding and marine engineering and celebrates acts of courage at sea. Also recounted are the exploits and achievements of Scots in all these fields, including those of James Watt, William Symington and Robert Stevenson.

Over the years many Scots have made their living and their fortunes from the sea, others have lost their lives to it – *Scots and the Sea* is a tribute to all of them.

James D.G. Davidson served as a naval officer in the Atlantic, the Pacific, the Mediterranean and the Persian Gulf. Present in Tokyo Harbour at the time of the Japanese surrender in 1945, he was Assistant Naval Attaché in Moscow at the time of Stalin's death.

ROUGH WATER

Stories of Survival from the Sea

Edited by Clint Willis

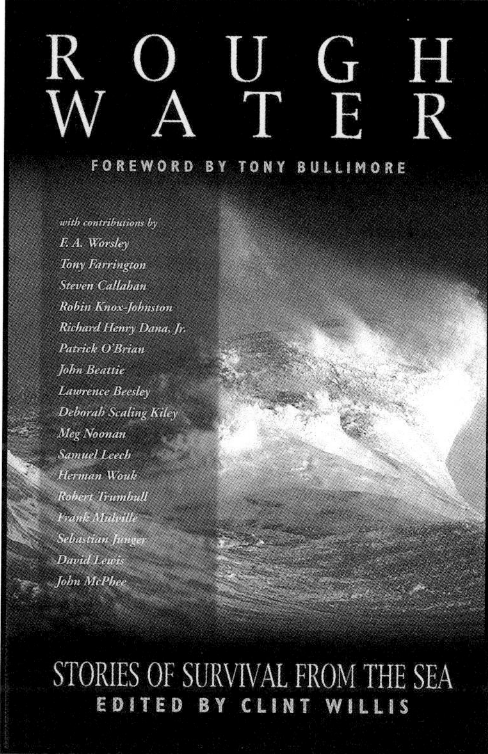

ISBN 1 84018 263 6
£9.99 (paperback)
Now available
234 x 156mm
368pp
b/w illustrations throughout
Action/Adventure

A collection of shocking seafaring tales. Contributors include Steven Callahan, John Beattie, Meg Noonan and Samuel Leech.

This edition contains a foreword by Tony Bullimore, who famously survived a shipwreck in the Southern Ocean.

'An eclectic seabag of yarns for a sailor's library . . . these stories evoke in compelling prose the timeless quest of mariners to survive the sea that is at once savage and majestic'
Sailing Magazine

STORM

Stories of Survival from Land, Sea and Sky

Edited by Clint Willis

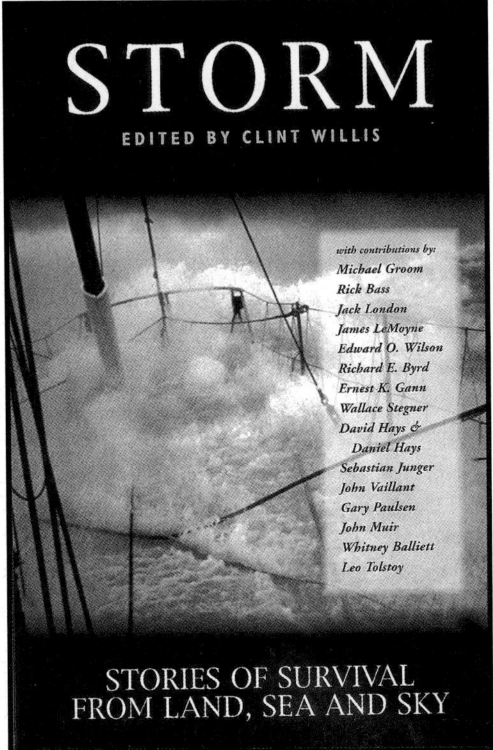

ISBN 1 84018 492 2
£9.99 (paperback)
Now available
234 x 156mm
306pp
b/w illustrations throughout
Action/Adventure

Sailors, climbers and other adventurers tell their stories of battling to stay alive while facing the full force of nature's fury. Contributors – including Jack London, Patrick O'Brien, John Muir and Leo Tolstoy – recount tales of human endurance, blizzards, typhoons, tornadoes and sandstorms.

Clint Willis is the editor of the *Adrenaline* series. He lives in Cape Elizabeth, USA.

THE MUNROS AND TOPS

A Record-Setting Walk in the Scottish Highlands

Chris Townsend

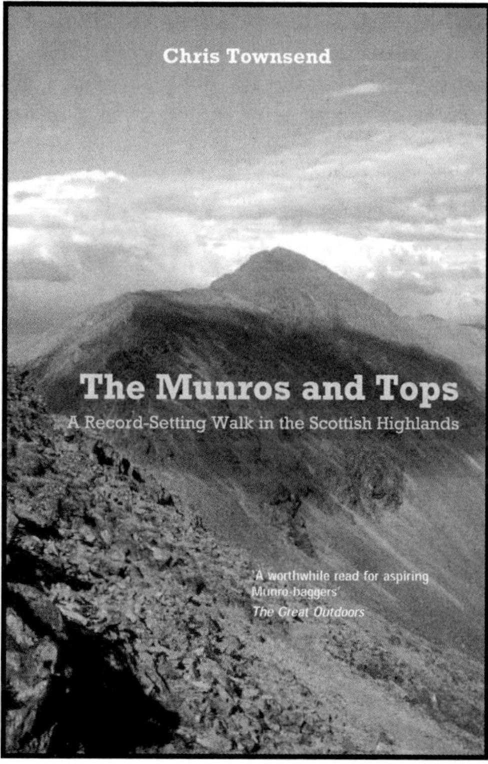

ISBN 1 84018 727 1
£9.99 (paperback)
April 2003
234 x 156mm
224pp
1 x 8pp colour
Climbing

When Chris Townsend reached the summit of Ben Hope in Sutherland, he walked his way into the record books. After 118 days in which he had covered more than 1,700 miles and climbed over 575,000 feet, he had completed the first single continuous journey of all 277 Munros and 240 Tops in the Scottish Highlands.

This is the story of that remarkable walk from the start on Ben More on the Isle of Mull through to the finish, the equivalent of climbing Mount Everest 18 times.

Illustrated with photographs taken during the walk, this is a stirring account of a unique achievement.

Chris Townsend is one of the world's most experienced long-distance wilderness walkers. His publication *The Backpacker's Handbook* won the Outdoor Writers Guild Award for Excellence in 1995.

'Well worth reading' Cameron McNeish

'A great read' *The Scottish Rambler*

THE GRAHAMS

A Guide to Scotland's 2,000ft Peaks

Andrew Dempster

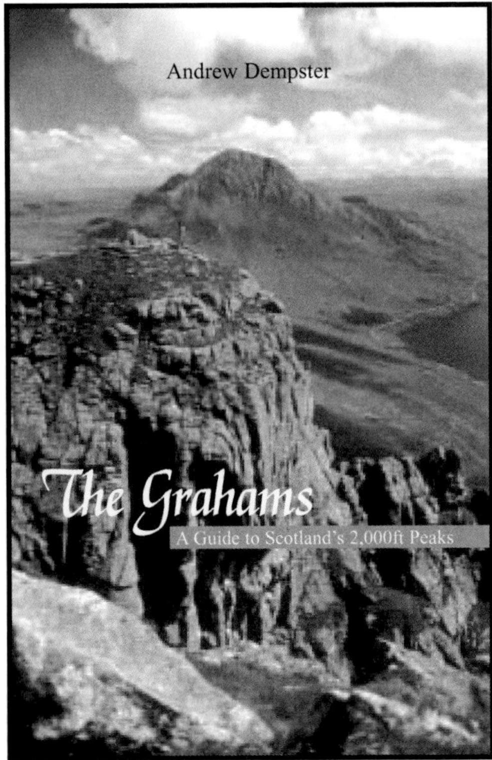

ISBN 1 84018 734 4
£9.99 (paperback)
April 2003
234 x 156mm
256pp
1 x 8pp colour,
b/w illustrations throughout
Guidebook

This thorough, well-illustrated guidebook is the first to describe the ascent of all Scottish mountains between 2,000 and 2,500 feet, collectively known as the Grahams. There are 224 such peaks scattered widely across the whole of the country. They range from remote rocky outcrops challenging the serious, seasoned hillwalker, to readily accessible hilltops for complete beginners. This book points the way to what could be considered the ultimate challenge for those who love Scotland's hills – the ascent of all 720 Munros, Corbetts and Grahams.

Andrew Dempster has had over 20 years' experience of walking in the Scottish mountains. His previous books include *Classic Mountain Scrambles in Scotland* and *The Munro Phenomenon.*